Day Walks on the South Downs

John Allen

"And along the sky the line of the Downs
So noble and so bare."
Hilaire Belloc: The South Country

Published by Sigma Leisure – an imprint of
Sigma Press, 1 South Oak Lane, Wilmslow, Cheshire SK9 6AR, England.

British Library Cataloguing in Publication Data
A CIP record for this book is available from the British Library.

ISBN: 1-85058-716-7

Typesetting and Design by: Sigma Press, Wilmslow, Cheshire.

Cover photograph: the author

Cover Design: MFP Design & Print

Photography: the author

Maps: Michael Gilbert

Printed by: MFP Design & Print

Disclaimer: the information in this book is given in good faith and is believed to be correct at the time of publication. No responsibility is accepted by either the author or publisher for errors or omissions, or for any loss or injury howsoever caused. Only you can judge your own fitness, competence and experience.

Preface

The South Downs provide the best walking in southern England. Rolling chalk hills give exhilarating walking with superb views and few obstructions. Unspoilt villages with beautiful old buildings, ancient churches and small, friendly inns snuggle at their foot. The Downs have an international reputation for their unique quality. They have long been an AONB, and, while this book was being prepared, it was proposed that they should become a National Park.

This book describes 31 walks, from Beacon Hill in Hampshire to Beachy Head in East Sussex. 28 give a full day's walking of five to six hours. A shorter alternative is suggested for those with less time or energy. Three half-day walks visit some out-of-the-way corners. Between them, the walks provide a thorough exploration of the area.

For each walk there is a detailed description of the route and a sketch map. Details are given of inns, restaurants and shops. Places of interest on the route are described, with details of opening times when appropriate. Information about maps, books and useful addresses is also included.

The preparation of this book has given me many deeply satisfying hours. I hope you will enjoy the walks as much as I have. Happy walking.

John Allen

Acknowledgements

I am grateful to Helen Slade, formerly South Downs Way Officer, and Jenny Grant, Monty Larkin and James Fisher of the Sussex Downs Conservation Board, who checked this work in draft and made several valuable suggestions. Martin Bond solved the mystery of the name of Glatting Beacon.

Dedication

This book is dedicated to all who have fought to protect the South Downs and the right of access to them.

Contents

The Walks

The South Downs

The Downs were formed beneath the sea, from the remains of countless billions of algae, though the exact process is still uncertain. An upheaval produced a vast dome of chalk over what is now south-east England, from which rivers ran to the sea. Then the top of the dome was eroded, leaving the ridges of the North and South Downs. Each ridge has a steep *escarpment*, which in the South Downs faces north. To the south there is a gentler *dip slope*. The softness of the chalk gives the Downs their gently rounded shape. A harder type of chalk creates a *secondary escarpment*, also north facing, in the vicinity of Worthing.

Chalk is porous. Water runs through it to emerge as clear springs at the foot of the escarpment – hence the chain of settlements here, and the small number of buildings on the Downs themselves. Dry river valleys, called *bottoms*, or *deans* (also *denes*), were formed in the Ice Age, when water could not escape into the frozen chalk and so carved channels through it. *Coombes*, "scoops" in the hillside, were also formed by the action of water. The natural cover of the Downs is not the famous turf, but trees and scrub – mainly gorse and hawthorn – which soon re-colonise idle ground.

The villages on the walks are all worth exploring for their old buildings. Lewes and Arundel are the only towns visited, although the coastal urban sprawl is often only too conspicuous. The churches are one of the great delights of the South Downs – as old and as simple as the faith of those who built them. Some are still lit by candles. Nearly all are left open for visitors (this may be assumed unless otherwise indicated), and most have an inexpensive guide for sale.

The Walks

Walking the South Downs is a never-failing delight. They have the feeling of openness and height given only by true hills. Long distances can be covered without consulting a map, negotiating gates and stiles or even changing direction. The going on the ridges is usually fairly level, but there are some stiff climbs up the escarpment and between the valleys – often after a good pub lunch. I have tried to provide a satisfying but not too strenuous day's walk of five to six hours, not including the lunch stop. Shorter options are suggested.

Most of the walks are hilly, and the ascent has a significant effect on the time taken. Because chalk drains rapidly, it does not produce deep mud, but it can be very slippery. Warning is given of particularly wet or muddy walks.

At an early stage in my fieldwork, I stopped noting all but the finest views. They are there nearly all the time – east and west along the ridge, south to the sea, and north over the Weald. The bottoms have a quieter, secluded beauty of their own.

Walkers are naturally curious about the identity of other areas of high ground, and the map on pages 6 and 7 has been included to satisfy this curiosity. Many of the paths and tracks are also bridleways, and riders and cyclists are frequently encountered. Motorcyclists may also be met, and, whatever personal views may be held, they have a legal right to use routes currently designated as a Road Used as a Public Path (RUPP). The Countryside Bill will allow an alternative re-classification, with routes designated as a footpath, a bridleway or a Byway Open to All Traffic (BOAT).

The **South Downs Way** features in many walks, because it follows the main ridge of the Downs and usually provides excellent walking. If you do all the walks in this book you will have done most of the Way, with the exception of short sections between the walks and the long western section between Winchester and Beacon Hill in Hampshire. The Way is the only National Trail which is also a bridleway, and it makes some odd detours to preserve this status – e.g. the long dog-leg round Beacon Hill near South Harting. Sensible walkers will take the direct route. At its eastern end, there are two routes between Alfriston and Eastbourne – the bridleway to the north and a footpath to the south.

Alfred Wainwright, doyen of guide book writers, concluded his classic seven volumes on the Lakeland Fells by listing his choice of "best" under various categories. I have done the same, and invite readers to compare their choice with mine. I have, with great difficulty, limited myself to six in each category. The order is alphabetical.

* **Best summits:** Beacon Hill (W Sussex); Bow Hill (above Kingley Vale); Cissbury Ring; Firle Beacon; Old Winchester Hill; Wolstonbury Hill.

* **Best views:** (very difficult) Amberley Mount; High and Over; Itford Hill; the Keymer Post; Mount Caburn; Seaford Head.

* **Best places to be (other than summits):** Chanctonbury Ring; The Devil's Dyke; Great Down (Slindon); The Long Man (Wilmington); The Seven Sisters; Standean Bottom.

Organisation

The Hampshire Downs – Walks 1 – 3

Walks 1 to 3 are entirely (and Walk 4 partly) in Hampshire. The Downs in this county lack the distinctive north-facing escarpment and its ridge, which end near the county boundary, and west of Beacon Hill (Hampshire) subside into gently rolling countryside. Nonetheless, the walking is excellent.

West of the Arun – Walks 4 – 12

The River Arun marks a change in the nature of the Downs. To the east they are mainly bare; to the west, thicker top-soils produce far more woodland (particularly noticeable when lots of little tree symbols have to be drawn on sketch maps). The walks in this area inevitably include quite a lot of this woodland – perhaps more than some walkers like.

East of the Arun – Walks 13 – 31

This is the area that many think of as the South Downs. The hills are mainly bare and afford the classic views that feature in so many paintings and photographs and, indeed, in the national consciousness. Many readers will share my view that the best walking is here.

East of the Cuckmere – Walks 25 – 28: a special note

The eastern end of the Downs is separated from the rest by the valley of the Cuckmere River. There are spectacular cliffs where the chalk meets the sea, long, high ridges, lovely bottoms and cool forests. I have squeezed in four walks in this area, and there is inevitably a little overlapping (you will get to know Jevington), but it would be unthinkable not to explore this magnificent area fully. Walks 25, 27 and 28 have a pub at both start and finish, and so can be done the other way round.

Contents of each walk

Title

Each walk has a number, which runs from west to east in order of the map reference of the starting point, and a list of the main points visited. The letter (L) indicates the recommended lunch stop. Walks 29 to 31 are half-day walks, and are in a separate west-east sequence.

Sections

Each paragraph describes a section of the walk, and has a number which cross-references it to the sketch map.

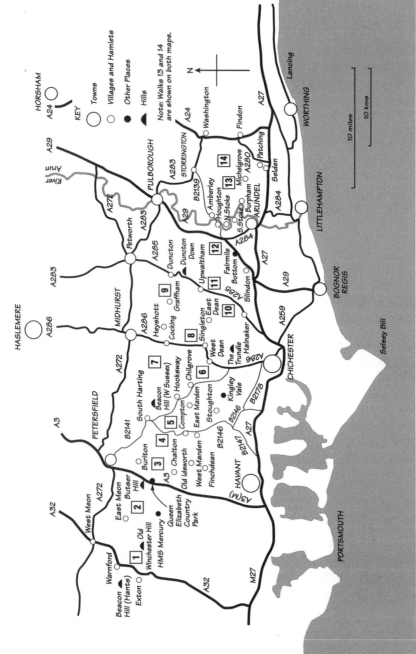

WALKS WEST OF THE ARUN

KEY

◯ Towns
○ Villages and Hamlets
● Other Places
▲ Hills

Note: Walks 13 and 14 are shown on both maps.

WALKS EAST OF THE ARUN

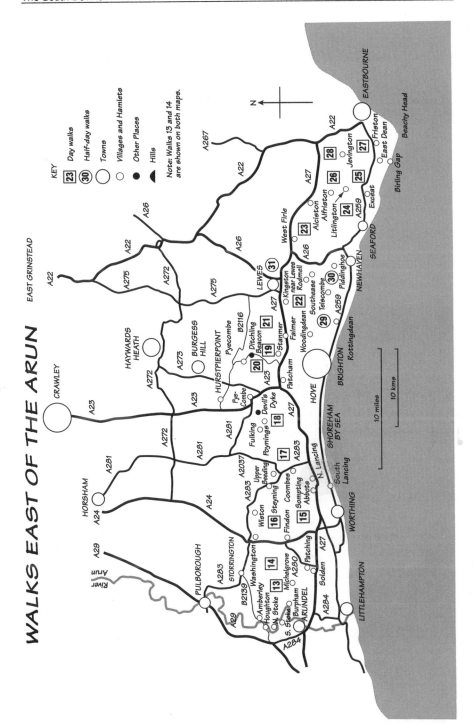

KEY

23	Day walks
30	Half-day walks
◯	Towns
○	Villages and Hamlets
●	Other Places
◣	Hills

Note: Walks 13 and 14 are shown on both maps.

THE SOUTH DOWNS AND NEIGHBOUR

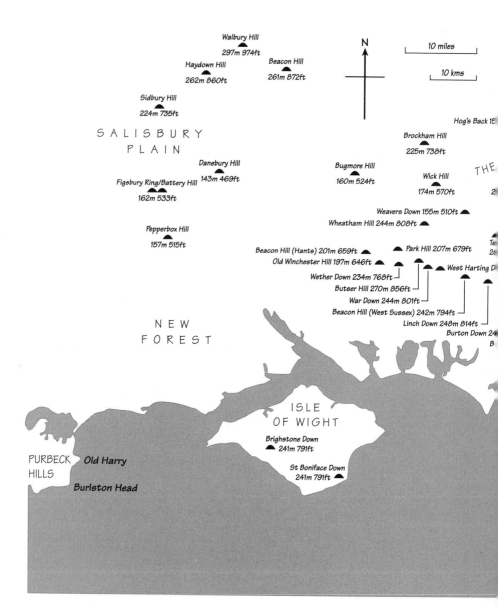

‍G HIGH GROUND

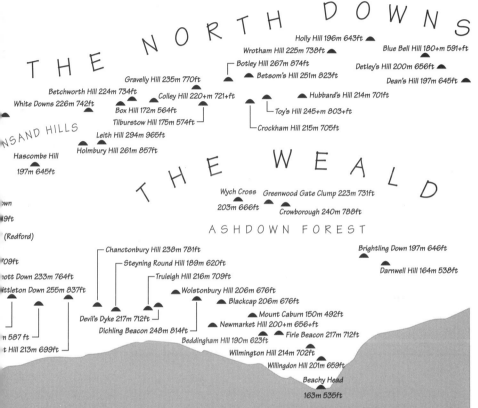

THE NORTH DOWNS

THE WEALD

Holly Hill 196m 643ft

Wrotham Hill 225m 738ft

Blue Bell Hill 180+m 591+ft

Botley Hill 267m 874ft

Detley's Hill 200m 656ft

Gravelly Hill 235m 770ft

Betsom's Hill 251m 823ft

Dean's Hill 197m 645ft

Betchworth Hill 224m 734ft

Colley Hill 220+m 721+ft

Hubbard's Hill 214m 701ft

White Downs 226m 742ft

Box Hill 172m 564ft

Toy's Hill 245+m 803+ft

Tilburstow Hill 175m 574ft

Crockham Hill 215m 705ft

‍NSAND HILLS

Leith Hill 294m 965ft

Hascombe Hill

Holmbury Hill 261m 857ft

197m 645ft

WYCH Cross

Greenwood Gate Clump 223m 731ft

203m 666ft

Crowborough 240m 788ft

ASHDOWN FOREST

‍own

‍9ft

(Redford)

Brightling Down 197m 646ft

‍709ft

Chanctonbury Hill 238m 781ft

Darnwell Hill 164m 538ft

‍nott Down 233m 764ft

Steyning Round Hill 189m 620ft

‍ittleton Down 255m 837ft

Truleigh Hill 216m 709ft

Wolstonbury Hill 206m 676ft

Blackcap 206m 676ft

Mount Caburn 150m 492ft

Devil's Dyke 217m 712ft

Newmarket Hill 200+m 656+ft

‍n 587 ft

Dichling Beacon 248m 814ft

Firle Beacon 217m 712ft

‍t Hill 213m 699ft

Beddingham Hill 190m 623ft

Wilmington Hill 214m 702ft

Willingdon Hill 201m 659ft

Beachy Head

163m 535ft

Notes:

The height in metres is taken from OS Landranger or Explorer maps. If neither of these gives a spot height for the summit, the highest contour has been used. This is indicated by a plus sign, e.g. 180+m. The triangulation pillar and the spot height are not always at the highest point.

The OS Travelmaster 1:250,000 map still, surprisingly, gives heights in feet, and the spot heights have been used when available. There are some discrepancies between these heights and those on the Landranger and Explorer maps. Otherwise, the height in feet has been obtained by multiplying the height in metres by 3.28084. As metres provide a less precise unit of measurement, this creates further minor discrepancies.

On many days the distant hills are hidden in haze (as on some days are the ones nearby). Few stand out distinctly from their surroundings; Blackdown being a notable exception, as befits the highest point in Sussex.

The following summits have view indicators: Old Winchester Hill, Beacon Hill (West Sussex), Devil's Dyke, High and Over.

Distances and ascent

Distances are given for the outward and return routes. The exact measurement in metres has (1) been rounded to the nearest half kilometre and (2) converted to miles and rounded to the nearest half mile. The ascent is given to the nearest five metres.

Times

Walking times are denoted in the form h:mm, for example 2:45 is 2 hours 45 minutes. It is difficult to give useful times for a walk. Different people walk at different speeds, and pace varies according to many factors, including fitness, fatigue, weather and ground conditions.

Naismith's Rule, in its metric version, states that a reasonably fit walker covers five kilometres (three miles) per hour on good level going. Each 10 metres (33 feet) of ascent requires another minute. This is an important consideration for most of the walks – 120 metres (393 feet) of ascent take as long as a level kilometre.

For most walkers, times calculated on this basis represent a minimum, because they do not allow for rests, map-reading, admiring the view, consulting the guide and getting lost. Adding 10% gives a fair approximation to my personal times, and this is the standard I have adopted. Times are based on the exact length of the walk, and have been rounded up to the nearest five minutes.

Readers are advised to record their own times, check them against the ones given, and establish a factor which can be used to adjust the times quoted to their personal performance.

Maps

Explorer and Landranger maps required for the walk are specified. Readers are strongly recommended to use an OS map in conjunction with this guide. **Landranger 1:50,000** (four maps): 185 Winchester & Basingstoke; 197 Chichester & The South Downs; 198 Brighton & Lewes; 199 Eastbourne and Hastings. **Explorer 1:25,000** (six maps); 119 Meon Valley & Portsmouth; 120 Chichester, South Harting & Selsey; 121 Arundel & Pulborough; 122 (17) South Downs Way – Steyning to Newhaven; 123 (18) South Downs Way – Newhaven to Eastbourne; 132 Winchester, New Alresford & East Meon. A number in brackets shows that the map has been renumbered, e.g. 122 was 17. Explorer maps have four times more space to show detail. The route followed on the ground is not always that shown on the map. This often occurs where walkers have taken a route more obvious than the right of way. Some footpath diversions are not shown on maps, but this is not necessarily the fault of the OS. A special symbol is used in the sketch maps for routes which differ from those on the map, and major divergences are mentioned in the text.

A single 1:40,000 scale map from Harveys shows the South Downs Way as a series of strips. It contains a great deal of useful information, but is of no use for the walks in this book.

Parking
A brief description and the map reference are given. Any charge is mentioned.

The walk
A brief description of the nature of the walk and its highlights.

Shorter walk(s)
Suggestions as to how the walk can be shortened without, as far as possible, missing the best features. Shorter routes are shown on the maps but are not arrowed.

Caution
About any hazards – usually mud or flood.

Route descriptions
A narrative description of the route is given. Many long stretches often need only a brief description, usually when following a ridge. Footpaths and bridleways which cross or diverge from the route are mentioned only if they provide a landmark, or if there is a risk of confusion. They are shown on the sketch maps.

Names of houses, farms, roads, etc. are given to help walkers check their position. Names shown on the ground are used when possible. Variants are indicated thus Dean (Dene?). On some parts of the Downs, there seems to be a dearth of names.

The word *continue* implies *in the same direction*. This should always be assumed; all major changes of direction are mentioned.

The appearance of a right of way can change drastically when a field is ploughed or put down to grass, or when the bareness of winter is replaced by the tall crops of summer.

Distances
The route descriptions include distances in metres, e.g. "Follow the edge of the field to a stile on the right (120m)". These are *approximate*, but should help in following the directions. Each distance is measured

from the preceding one. If there is a group of buildings, e.g. a farm, the distance is to the first.

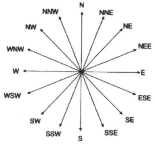

Compass directions

Compass directions are included when doubt may exist. Most readers will be familiar with the 16 points used, but the accompanying diagram is included in case a reminder is needed.

Bold letters

Important points on the walk are in bold type, e.g. **Lower Standean** or *Saddlescombe* (see En Route below).

Refreshments

The walks have been planned to include a lunch stop near the halfway point. This is usually an inn (the word does not imply that accommodation is available), but restaurants, etc. are mentioned when present. Many inns are effectively licensed restaurants at weekends, and it is possible to arrive at 12.30 to find the place almost empty, but a *Reserved* sign on every table. Booking is often essential if a meal is required, and for these inns the telephone number is given. Other places of refreshment along the walk are also mentioned.

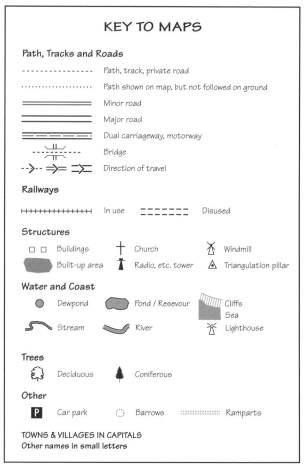

KEY TO MAPS

Path, Tracks and Roads

- - - - - - - - - - - - - - - Path, track, private road
· Path shown on map, but not followed on ground
═══════════ Minor road
═══════════ Major road
═ ═ ═ ═ ═ ═ ═ Dual carriageway, motorway
- - - ⊥⊥ - - - - Bridge
- - > - - ⇒ = ⊃⊂ Direction of travel

Railways

⊢⊣⊢⊣⊢⊣⊢⊣⊢⊣⊢⊣ In use   ═ ═ ═ ═ ═ ═ ═ Disused

Structures

□ □ Buildings   † Church   ✕ Windmill
▬ Built-up area   ▮ Radio, etc. tower   △ Triangulation pillar

Water and Coast

● Dewpond   Pond / Resevour   Cliffs / Sea
Stream   River   Lighthouse

Trees

🌳 Deciduous   🌲 Coniferous

Other

🅿 Car park   ⋰ Barrows   ▓▓▓ Ramparts

TOWNS & VILLAGES IN CAPITALS
Other names in small letters

Shops

Are mentioned if present, but are not to be found on many walks.

En route

Under this heading notes about places of interest are given at the end of each walk. To indicate their presence, the name in the route description is italicised, e.g. *Saddlescombe*. Much has had to be left out because of space; for further information see the book list.

Sketch map

A sketch map is provided of each walk. The scale of these is usually 1:50,000, but has sometimes been reduced to avoid a split. Some features have been exaggerated to make them clearer. The suggestion is repeated that OS maps should be used as well as this guide.

Abbreviations

m/r denotes map reference; NT: National Trust; OS: Ordnance Survey; RoW: Right of Way; SDW: South Downs Way.

Books

Walking Guides

South Downs Way

There must be more guides to the South Downs Way than to any other footpath in the country.

A Guide to the South Downs Way*: Miles Jebb, Constable, 1984; route descriptions in both directions. A wealth of information about places on or near the SDW.

Along the South Downs Way: Harry Comber; Society of Sussex Downsmen, 1998; route descriptions in both directions. A small, inexpensive but excellent guide.

South Downs Way: National Trail Guide, Paul Millmore; Aurum Press, 1990; route description east to west. Everything walkers, cyclists and riders tackling the Way need to know.

The South Downs Way*: Aerofilms Guide, Ian Allan, 1992; aerial photographs of the Way, guide and directions.

The South Downs Way Notebook: R. and S. Mills (also publishers), 1999; route description west to east. All done by hand, pocket-sized.

South Downs Way and the Downs Link: K. Reynolds, Cicerone; route descriptions in both directions. A handy pocket-sized guide.

Others

Stroll the South Downs: NT; family walks to eight NT sites in Sussex, up to 4½ miles.

Pub Walks in the South Downs: Ben Perkins; Countryside Books, 1996; 14 short walks.

General

Countless books have been published. The following are those I have found most useful or interesting. Books tend to concentrate on the eastern Downs.

The South Downs: Peter Brandon, Phillimore, 1998; a comprehensive history and modern overview. Expensive, but every lover of the Downs should have it.

Along the South Downs*: David Harrison, Cassell, 1958; still a treasure trove of information.

Ancient Churches of Sussex: Ken & Joyce Whiteman, 1994, S.B. Publications.

The Hidden Places of Sussex: Barbara Vesey (ed.), 1998, Travel Publishing; in spite of its title, a useful general guide, with the emphasis on accommodation and food.

A History of Sussex: Roy Armstrong, Phillimore, 1995 (fourth edition); particularly good on buildings.

The Landscape of the Sussex Downs: Countryside Commission/South Downs Conservation Board, 1996; a detailed analysis of the different types of landscape.

Nature in Downland*: W.H. Hudson, 1900; a classic portrait of the Downs a century ago.

South Downs*: Ordnance Survey Leisure Guide, AA & OS, 1988; Butser Hill to Eastbourne; maps, colour photos, lots of information.

The South Downs*: Ben Darby, Hale, 1976; a loving, knowledgeable and well-written account.

The South Downs: Michael George, Pavilion, 1997; colour photographs of the Brighton-Lewes-Eastbourne triangle.

Sussex: David J Allen; Shire County Guide, 1995; covers East and West Sussex.

Sussex Place Names: Judith Glover, Countryside Books, 1997; many names do not mean what they appear to.

* out of print at time of going to press

Video

Discovering the South Downs, 1997; Gaia Video Communications.

Useful addresses and telephone numbers

The Society of Sussex Downsmen: 10, The Drive, Hove, East Sussex, BN3 2BA; tel: 01273 771906 (09.30-12.30 only). The society works to protect the Downs and the right of access. It organises social activities, including numerous walks, and publishes a quarterly newsletter. The annual subscription is modest, and all who enjoy the Downs are urged to join.

County Councils

East Sussex County Council: Sackville House, Brooks Close, Lewes, East Sussex, BN7 1VE; tel: 01273 481000

West Sussex County Council: County Hall, Chichester, West Sussex, PO19 1RL; tel: 01243 777100.

Hampshire County Council: Mottisfount Court, High Street, Winchester, SO23 8ZB; tel: 01962 870500.

Outdoor organisations

The Camping and Caravanning Club, Greenfields House, Westwood Way, Coventry, CV4 8JH; tel: 01203 694995.

The Caravan Club: East Grinstead House, East Grinstead, West Sussex, RH19 1UA; tel: 01342 326944.

The Ramblers Association: 1/5 Wandsworth Road, London SW8 2XX; tel: 0171 339 8500.

The Youth Hostels Association: Trevelyan House, 8 St Stephen's Hill, St Albans, Herts., AL1 2DY; tel: 01727 855215. There are hostels at Alfriston, Arundel, Brighton, Eastbourne, Telscombe and Truleigh Hill.

Tourist Board

South East England Tourist Board: The Old Brew House, Warwick Park, Tunbridge Wells, Kent, TN2 5TU; tel: 01892 540766.

Tourist Information Centres

West Sussex

Burgess Hill: 96 Church Walk, RH15 9AS; tel: 01444 247726
Chichester: 29a South Street, PO19 1AH; tel: 01243 775888.

East Sussex

Brighton: 10 Bartholomew Square, BN1 1JS; tel: 01273 292599.
Hove: Church Road, BN3 3BQ; tel: 01273 292589.
Lewes: 187 High Street; tel: 01273 483448.
Boship: Lower Dicker, Hailsham; tel: 01323 332667.

Hampshire:

Petersfield: County Library, The Square, GU32 3HH; tel: 01730 268829.

Countryside Centres and Parks:

Beachy Head Countryside Centre: (Walk 27) Eastbourne, East Sussex, BN20 7YA; tel: 01323 737273

Queen Elizabeth Country Park: (Walk 2) Gravel Hill, Horndean, Waterlooville, Hampshire, PO8 0QE; tel: 02392 597618.

Seven Sisters Country Park: (Walk 25) Exceat, Seaford, East Sussex, BN25 4AD; tel: 01323 870280 (winter opening: weekends only (11.00-16.00)

Other

Sussex Downs Conservation Board: Chanctonbury House, Church Street, Storrington, West Sussex RH20 4LT; tel: 01903 741234.

East Hampshire AONB Officer: Queen Elizabeth Country Park, Gravel Hill, Horndean, Waterlooville, PO8 0QE; tel: 02392 597618.

South Downs Way Officer: Queen Elizabeth Country Park, Gravel Hill, Horndean, Waterlooville, PO8 0QE; tel: 02392 597618.

Glossary

AONB: Area of Outstanding Natural Beauty. The South Downs consists of two such areas – Sussex Downs and East Hampshire (see useful names and addresses).

Barrow: a burial mound, usually called *tumuli* on OS maps. *Long barrows* are neolithic; *round barrows* are Bronze Age. *Bowl barrows* are closely surrounded by a ditch; *bell barrows* have a ditch separated from the mound by a flat area. A hollow in the top is a sign of excavation, usually in the XVIII and XIX centuries.

Beacon: the term occurs frequently – e.g. Beacon Hill, Ditchling Beacon – and indicates that a prominent top was once used for beacon fires.

Bostal: a track up the escarpment.

Chalk pits and quarries: to reduce the acidity of the topsoil, chalk, a pure form of limestone, was dug and spread, and the pits thus produced are still visible. There are also many large and often unsightly quarries.

Clunch: (lovely word) a hard form of chalk, sometimes used for building.

Dencher: land reclaimed for agriculture. Sometimes mystifyingly corrupted to *denture*.

Dew ponds: the water problem led to the construction of these ponds, lined with impervious clay. In spite of their name, they depend on rain. Many are in disrepair.

Dyke: many earthworks are labelled *Cross Dyke* on OS maps. They are thought to have marked the boundaries of grazing land.

ESA: Environmentally Sensitive Area. Most of the Downs is so classified. Farmers are paid by MAFF to conserve the traditional grassland and wildlife, by not using fertilisers, restricting the use of pesticides, reverting arable to pasture, and managing grazing to restrict the spread of scrub. 70% of the downland is covered by these voluntary agreements.

Farming: because the light soils were relatively easy to clear and work with primitive tools (c.f. the heavy clays of the Weald), they were brought into cultivation early. That is why there are so many ancient remains.

For many centuries the traditional farming method was a mixture of pasture and arable. Sheep were grazed on the high ground during the day, and driven down at night to dung and trample the arable fields. The famous Southdown breed was developed for this method, but was too fatty for modern tastes and is now rare.

It is widely believed that the high Downs were predominantly grazing land until the Second World War, during and just after which they were ploughed to provide desperately needed grain. Recent research, however, indicates that in some areas at least arable use has always been common when market forces dictated. Be that as it may, much of the downland is now under the plough. Wheat, barley and oilseed rape are grown, and cattle as well as sheep are grazed. Llama and buffalo may also be seen.

Flint: a rock of almost pure silica, which occurs in chalk. In Neolithic times arrowheads and tools such as knives and scrapers were made. To obtain a better quality, mines were dug which still pockmark many hilltops. Later, flint was widely used for houses and farm buildings. *Knapped* flint is shaped, revealing its dark, glossy interior.

Forts: are found on most hilltops. "Fortified enclosures" is a better description. They date from the Iron Age and are so common that they are not always mentioned in route descriptions. The word *Ring* in a name usually indicates their presence.

Hanger: a hanging wood on a steep slope, usually the escarpment.

Hovel: a shelter for farm animals.

Lynchet: the edge of an old field. Ploughing and rain moved soil from the top of a field to the bottom, creating a raised bank at the edge. Many old field systems can be seen on the Downs.

Place names: most names are of Saxon origin, and many simply record an owner – e.g. Alfriston was *Aelfric's tun* (farmstead). They can be confusing – I have walked unnecessary miles through confusing Litlington and Lullington. Alciston and Alfriston, Iford and Itford and Patcham and Patching are other examples.

Duplication also occurs. In West Sussex the two villages of West Dean and East Dean are near to each other, as are Westdean and East Dean in East Sussex. There are Beacon Hills in Hampshire (two) and West Sussex, a Mount Harry near Brighton and another near Lewes. New Barns are common (and always old).

Pronunciation: Pronunciation seems to be changing. For example, many books state that Alciston is pronounced Arlston, but locals inform me that the obvious form is now being used.

Sea: in mediaeval times, the sea extended much further inland and many places, now miles inland, were ports. There is an old beach near Slindon.

Telegraph: high points were used for telegraph signalling towers, and this is recorded in the names of hills and houses.

Tumuli: see *Barrow*.

Turf: densely textured, springy turf was created by centuries of grazing by sheep and rabbits. It supports a great variety of plant life, and conservation bodies seek to preserve and restore it. Only 5% now remains, mainly on slopes too steep for the plough. There is a vivid description of downland turf in W.H. Hudson's *A Shepherd's Life*: "The sheep fed closely, and everything that grew on the down – grasses, clovers, and small creeping herbs – had acquired the habit of growing and flowering close to the ground, every species and every individual plant striving, with the unconscious intelligence that is in all growing things, to hide its leaves and pushing sprays under the others, to escape the nibbling teeth by keeping closer to the surface."

Twitten: a narrow path.

Walk 1

Old Winchester Hill, Beacon Hill (Hampshire), Warnford (L), West Meon

Distances: out 11.5 km, 7.0 miles; return 10.0 km, 6.5 miles

Ascent: out 165m; return 255m

Times: out 2:50; return 2:45

Maps: Explorer 119, Landranger 185

Parking: car park on Old Winchester Hill (m/r 645214). The park further south (m/r 647208) is for the disabled.

The walk: in the Hampshire Downs, individual summits are more distinct. This walk visits two of the best-known, and explores part of the Meon Valley. The distances and timings assume a lunch stop at Warnford, but West Meon, about 35 minutes further on, is an alternative.

Shorter walk: from West Meon, follow the road to Coombes Lane. Turn right and follow the lane to Whitewool Farm.

Caution: in wet conditions the section of the SDW along Garden Hill Lane, between Monarch's Way (m/r 633213) and the A32 (m/r 617212) is better described as the South Downs Wade. Flooding can make it impassable unless walkers have really waterproof boots and are prepared to risk wet feet. A way of avoiding the worst is described. Elsewhere slippery mud makes progress slow and frustrating. *Note: as this book was going to press, proposals were made for a new route for the SDW between Garden Hill Lane and the car park on Beacon Hill.*

---

1. From the car park walk a few steps up to the ridge and turn left along a grassy path. Follow it round to the right beside the road to join a track (700m), and continue to gates. Take the one on the right, and turn left and right along the ridge to the summit of *Old Winchester Hill* (1,050m).

2. Continue down the west ridge, through downland, a wood, and fields. At the bottom of a field turn right (650m). The map may incorrectly show the SDW continuing westwards down the ridge. Follow a path through a zigzag along the edges of fields, and move left (550m) to join a track. At a junction (100m), turn left along a track which often doubles as a stream, and soon shrinks to a path. Initially it may be necessary to wade along the path/stream later there are higher paths on one side or the other.

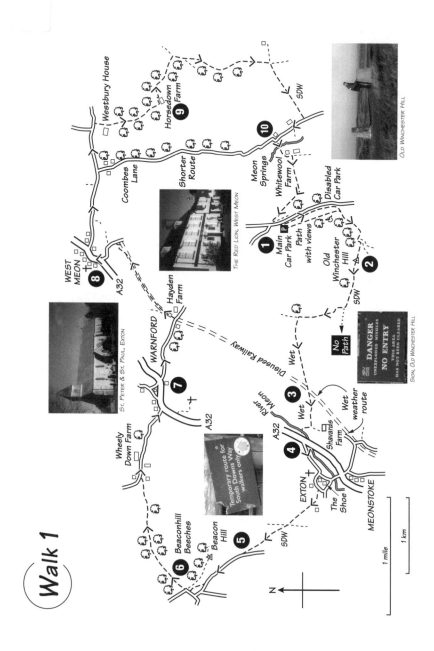

Walk 1

THE RED LION, WEST MEON

ST. PETER & ST. PAUL, EXTON

OLD WINCHESTER HILL

SIGN, OLD WINCHESTER HILL

DANGER
UNEXPLODED MISSILES
NO ENTRY
THIS AREA
HAS NOT BEEN CLEARED

Temporary route for
South Downs Way
walkers only

Westbury House

Horsedown
Farm 9

Coombes
Lane

Shorter
Route

Meon
Springs

Whitewool
Farm

Disabled
Car Park

10

SDW

WEST
MEON 8

A32

WARNFORD

Hayden
Farm

Main
Car Park 1

Path
with views

Old
Winchester
Hill 2

SDW

No
Path

Wet

Disused Railway

River
Meon

Wet

3

Wet
weather
route

Shavards
Farm

Wheely
Down Farm

7

A32

A32

4

EXTON

The
Shoe

MEONSTOKE

Beaconhill
Beeches

6

Beacon
Hill 5

SDW

N

1 mile

1 km

3. Go over or under the old railway (900m) and continue. The worst floods can be missed by turning left along the former embankment, and then right along a lane to Exton (see map). Continue to a junction by **Shavards Farm** on the left (500m), where the flooding is usually worst, and turn right. Follow a path round to the left and cross the River Meon by a footbridge.

4. Cross the A32 (180m) and follow a lane to *Exton*. Go round to the right past the church (600m), opposite which a lane on the left leads to the inn. Continue round to the left and just past Glebe Cottage (150m) take a path on the right, cross a stile and continue along the edge of a field. Follow the hedge round to the right, cross a stile (200m) and continue diagonally NW across a field to its far corner. Continue across the next field along a faint path. Cross a private "road" (400m), bear a little to the right and continue diagonally uphill through a field to a stile about a third of the way along its right-hand edge. Cross the corner of the next field aiming for a yellow disc, go through a strip of woodland and steeply across two more fields to a lane (750m).

5. There is no direct access to Beacon Hill from here, so turn right along the lane. At the high point (500m), take a path on the right across the corner a field, which leads to a car park (300m) (if muddy, follow the lane). To visit the summit of *Beacon Hill*, turn sharply back to the right along a track and walk past Beaconhill Beeches to the triangulation pillar (550m).

6. Return to the car park (550m) and turn right along a path going gently downhill (NE) through a wood into a field (300m). Bear gently round to the right, past a wood on the left (600m) (there were plantings here in 1999 that would extend this wood to both sides of the path). Continue down to the bottom of a field, take a gate on the right (350m) and turn left along a track. Follow this through **Wheely Down Farm** to a road (250m) and turn right. Continue to the A32 (900m) and turn left into *Warnford* (250m). Follow the A32 through the village to the inn (250m).

7. **Return:** just past the inn, take a lane on the right signposted *Clanfield* (50m). Follow it over the brow of a hill to a bridge over the disused Meon Valley Railway (900m). Turn left just before the parapet, and follow a path to an old style (80m). Descend to the cutting (90m), turn left and follow the course of the old line to a turning cir-

cle (800m). Follow a track to a lane (250m), turn left and walk into **West Meon** (250m).

8. Turn right along the A32 (150m), then take a road on the right sign-posted *East Meon* (200m). Pass **Coombe Lane** on the right (1,050m) and continue to the drive to **Westbury House** on the right (600m). Follow the drive until it swings right to the house (150m) and keep straight on to a gate and stile. Bear slightly right and go uphill between old gateposts into a wood. Follow a path which winds a little but generally goes SSE. Continue over a stile (300m). When a field appears on the right, take a gate (or stile) on the left (500m). Turn left and follow a path round to the right through woodland below **Horsedown Farm** (80m).

9. Go through a kissing gate and turn left along the edge of a field. At its corner continue down steps and turn right (180m) along a track. Where the track swings right take a path on the left (300m). Cross a style on the left (40m) and turn right steeply downhill along the edges of two fields. Turn right along a track (300m) and keep left at gates (120m). Continue S to a crossing track, the SDW, by farm buildings on the left (1,300m) and turn right. Continue SW to a lane (850m) and turn right.

10. Where the lane turns right (450m), turn left along a private road to **Whitewool Farm**. Cross the bridge over Meon Springs Fly Fishery, and follow the road round to the left, keeping the farm buildings on the left. At a T-junction by the farm buildings (300m), turn right. Follow a track W to the foot of a hill by an old quarry (400m), and bear right along.a track which makes an ascending traverse of the hill to a lane (550m). Turn sharp back left to the car park (180m).

En route

Old Winchester Hill: is a long way from Winchester. It is a National Nature Reserve, and very popular. The summit has a triangulation pillar, a view indicator and a superb view which includes the Isle of Wight.

Exton: the chancel of the CHURCH OF ST PETER & ST PAUL is at a slight angle to the nave. Nobody know why. The inn is THE SHOE.

Beacon Hill: is usually regarded as the western end of the South Downs, although the SDW continues to Winchester. There is another Beacon Hill in West Sussex (Walk 7).

Warnford: the whole village was moved when a new road was built

The view to Exton from Old Winchester Hill

during the Napoleonic Wars, which is why the CHURCH OF OUR LADY is so far away. The inn is THE GEORGE AND FALCON.

West Meon: THE CHURCH OF ST JOHN THE EVANGELIST is surprisingly large. It has some fine knapped flint and a peal of eight bells. There are old houses in many different styles, as well as shops. There are two inns, THE RED LION and THE THOMAS LORD, the latter named after the founder of the London cricket ground, who retired to the village.

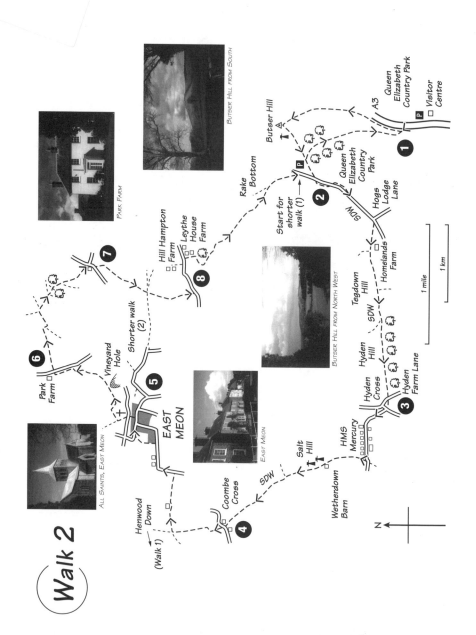

Walk 2

QUEEN ELIZABETH COUNTRY PARK
A3
Visitor Centre
P
①
Butser Hill
Queen Elizabeth Country Park
P
Hogs Lodge Lane
②
SDW
Rake Bottom
Start for shorter walk (1)
BUTSER HILL FROM SOUTH
Homelands Farm
Tegdown Hill
SDW
Hyden Hill
Leythe House Farm
Hill Hampton Farm
⑧
Homelands Farm
BUTSER HILL FROM NORTH WEST
Hyden Cross
Hyden Farm Lane
③
1 km
1 mile
⑦
Shorter walk (2)
Vineyard Hole
⑤
EAST MEON
HMS Mercury
Salt Hill
Wetherdown Barn
SDW
⑥
Park Farm
PARK FARM
ALL SAINTS, EAST MEON
Henwood Down
(Walk 1)
Coombe Cross
④
EAST MEON
N

Walk 2

Butser Hill, HMS Mercury, East Meon (L)

Distances: out 11.0 km, 7.0 miles; return 9.5 km, 6.0 miles

Ascent: out 210m; return 250m

Times: out 2:50; return 2:35

Maps: Explorer 119, 120, Landranger 185, 197

Parking: Queen Elizabeth Country Park (m/r 717185) on the A3 (moderate charge). There is free parking at a lay-by on the A3 N of the start (m/r 718190).

The walk: the first section of the walk ascends Butser Hill and follows the SDW along a series of tracks and lanes. The return explores the attractive village of East Meon and some pleasantly varied countryside.

Shorter walks: 1. the initial ascent of Butser Hill may be avoided by using a car park near the summit (moderate charge) (m/r 711200). 2. from East Meon, walk E along a lane and a track (see map).

---

1. Go under the A3 bridge (from which the distances are measured) and follow the SDW round to the right. Two ridges are visible. The one on the left (the SDW) is used on the return; the outward route ascends the one on the right. Take a path on the left and follow it round to the right, between a metalled track and the A3. Continue along the old road and where it ends bear left along a track, still beside the A3, and cross a stile by a gate. Cross another stile (550m) then bear left up **Butser Hill**. Continue over a stile to the triangulation pillar (1,300m) – the final section is almost pathless. From the summit, go to the left of the radio tower along a grassy path. Join a track, follow it SW, and join a road by a car park. Where it bends right (450m), keep straight on along a path and follow it to rejoin the road. (400m).

2. Continue along the road. Pass a lane on the right (400m) and continue to a junction with a road sign *Hogs Lodge Lane* (500m). Bear right along a metalled track and follow it W past Homelands Farm (280m), where it becomes unmade. Continue over **Tegdown Hill** and **Hyden Hill** to a road junction at **Hyden Cross** (1,950m).

3. Keep straight on along a road signposted *Droxford*. Continue over another junction at Hyden Farm Lane (100m) and follow the road round to the right and past **HMS Mercury**. Just past the buildings turn right along a track (800m) and continue past Wetherdown Barn (600m). Continue NNW over Salt Hill to a lane at **Coombe Cross** (1,600m).

4. Cross the lane and follow a track through a zigzag to a junction of tracks below Henwood Down, visited on Walk 1 (750m). Turn right and follow a path E between fields and a zigzag past barns on the left. Join a concrete track (350m) and continue to a road (400m). Turn left and follow the road round to the right (200m). Take Duncombe Road on the left (300m) and keep straight on to the road end. Housing developments here may not be shown on the map. Continue along a path across a field, bear right past the village hall to a road (300m), and turn right into *East Meon*. At a junction of roads continue into the village centre (200m).

5. **Return:** walk N to the church (100m) and take a path just to its left. Bear left above the graveyard and continue uphill. Just before a stile, ascend steps on the right to another stile (170m). Go steeply uphill by an old hedge, cross a stile and turn right along the edge of a field (180m) with a fence on the right. Cross a stile on the right and continue along a path which contours the hillside, with the fence now on the left. Go above **Vineyard Hole** (450m) and follow the fence round to the left. At a

The track above Park Farm

hedge (650m) go downhill to a gate and stile and continue along the bottom of a field to **Park Farm** (250m) and a lane.

6. Cross and follow a track ENE uphill. Just over the brow of the hill follow the track round to the right (550m) and then turn left (80m) downhill with a hedge on the left. At the bottom of the field (200m)

turn right along a track, and follow it past a footpath on the left.
Some of the tracks in the next section may not appear on the map.
Where another track crosses (230m), at the edge of a wood, keep
straight on over a grass triangle and down a steep path (20m), to join
a track going steeply downhill through a wood. At the bottom of the
hill (250m) leave the more obvious track and continue downhill
through a broken gate (40m) along a grassy path on the left. Continue along the lower edge of a field to a T-junction of roads by a cottage (500m) and turn right.

7. Where the road bends right take a track on the left (90m). Where the
    track swings left into a field (350m) continue SW along a path. At a
    junction of paths (450m) keep straight on, going slightly uphill at
    first. Continue to a lane (650m) and turn left. Just past **Hill Hampton
    Farm** (400m), take a track (Limekiln Lane) on the right (60m).

8. Where the track ends at a cottage, continue along a sunken path and
    begin the second ascent of **Butser Hill**. Follow the track right and
    left and continue SE uphill. Rake Bottom, which appears on the left,
    is reminiscent of The Devil's Dyke. At a lane at the top (2,300m),
    turn sharply back to the left to the car park. Where the lane swings
    left (150m), keep straight on along the grassy path used on the out-
    ward route. Bear right to a gate and bear right again to another
    (250m). Walk down the ridge and beside the A3 to rejoin the out-
    ward route to the A3 bridge (1,200).

En route

The Queen Elizabeth Country Park: has a visitor centre, toilets and
café. The ANCIENT FARM PROJECT, which may be shown on the map near
the start of the walk, has moved elsewhere – see Walk 3.

Butser Hill: at 270m, is the highest point on the South Downs. The view
includes five counties. BLACKDOWN, the highest point in Sussex, can be
seen to the NE. There are toilets.

HMS Mercury: a closely guarded R.N. communications school. Just
past its first car park are the remains of an Iron Age earthwork

East Meon: is featured on the 1998 Explorer map. The RIVER MEON
flows through the village, which has many old buildings. ALL SAINTS
CHURCH, with its spire and roof of white lead, dominates the area. Its famous Tournai font was made in Flanders in the XII century. There are
two inns, YE OLD GEORGE and THE IZAAK WALTON, and a village stores.

Walk 3

Windmill Hill, Finchdean (L), Chalton

Distances: out 10.5 km, 6.5 miles; return 8.0 km, 5.0 miles

Ascent: out 175m; return 210m

Times: out 2:40; return 2:10

Maps: Explorer 120, Landranger 197

Parking: car park half a kilometre SW of Buriton (m/r 733198) on the road to Finchdean.

The walk: is pleasantly varied, with woodland, farmland, downland and two attractive villages. A visit to Butser Ancient Farm on the outward leg is recommended.

Shorter walk: start at the car park at the Queen Elisabeth Country Park Visitor Centre (see Walk 2). On the return, turn left inside the Park and follow the edge of the forest back.

---

1. For the first section, SDW signs can be followed. From the car park take a track going initially NW, and follow it uphill and round to the left into the **Queen Elizabeth Country Park**. Shortly after a track joins from the right (650m) keep right at a fork (80m) signposted *SDW Walkers*. Go gently downhill through woodland and continue SW through a car park to a hairpin bend in a metalled road (1,100m). Take a path on the left (50m) and follow it beside the road. Continue past another car park towards the A3. Turn left uphill (500m), leaving the SDW, along a track (for the Visitor Centre, turn right).

2. Take a track on the right (90m) and follow it parallel to the A3, with forest on the left and fields on the right. At the track bears away from the A3, the Chalton Windmill appears on the right. Where the track swings left, there is a wooden seat (950m). Cross a stile on the right, which is not obvious, turn left along a path and follow it S between fences to a lane (700m).

3. Turn right and cross a stile on the left (40m). Turn right again and follow a path gradually away from the road. Cross the track (150m) to *Butser Ancient Farm*, continue uphill and cross a stile by the A3 (450m). Turn left along a private road and follow it uphill to the **Chalton Windmill** on **Windmill Hill** (700m).

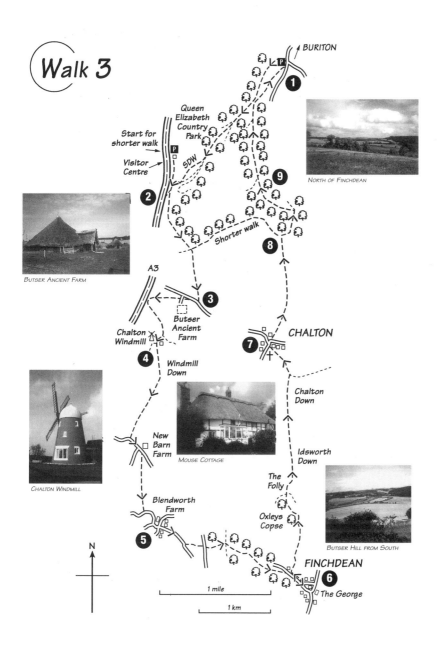

Walk 3

BURITON

Queen
Elizabeth
Country
Park

Start for
shorter walk

Visitor
Centre

SDW

Shorter walk

NORTH OF FINCHDEAN

BUTSER ANCIENT FARM

A3

Butser
Ancient
Farm

Chalton
Windmill

CHALTON

Windmill
Down

Chalton
Down

New
Barn
Farm

MOUSE COTTAGE

Idsworth
Down

The
Folly

CHALTON WINDMILL

Blendworth
Farm

Oxleys
Copse

BUTSER HILL FROM SOUTH

FINCHDEAN

N

1 mile

1 km

The George

4. Continue along a track with the windmill on the right, and follow it round to the left. Continue along the edge of a field and go S and then SW down the ridge of Windmill Down to a lane (1,400m), and turn left to **New Barn Farm**. Keep left in front of the farm (170m) and, just past it, take a path on the right (100m). Cross a large field to the left of a pylon, and continue S along the edge of a smaller field to a lane (800m). Turn left past **Blendworth Farm**.

5. Keep left at a junction (130m), left again at the next, and right at the next. Where the lane bends right take a path on the left (500m) along the edge of a field to a lane (280m). Cross and continue along the edge of a field, with a wood on the left. At a corner bear slightly left across the field to a stile (280m). Go into a wood, cross a track and turn right along a footpath (20m). Follow the path through the wood, over crossing tracks and past a field. At a T-junction (300m) turn left and follow a path round to the right. Descend SE to a lane (700m) and turn right. The return walk can be started here. Keep right by Ashcroft Lane and continue to the inn (450m).

6. **Return:** the return follows the Staunton Way into the Queen Elizabeth Country Park, and the waymarks are useful. From the inn walk back along the lane. By Ashcroft Lane take a stile on the right (250m) and follow a path beside the road. At the corner of the field (180m) turn right uphill and follow its edge up onto the ridge. Go through Oxleys Copse and turn left (800m) and then right (80m) along the ridge. Follow the winding edge of the field, with woodland on the left. Continue past The Folly (500m) (of which there is no sign) and continue N along the ridge. Take a stile on the left (200m) and continue, following marker posts, over **Idsworth Down** and past tumuli on the summit of **Chalton Down** (500m). Descend towards **Chalton** (see Walk 4), still following marker posts. Cross a stile (1,000m) and bear left down to the church. Go through the graveyard to the Red Lion (300m).

7. Turn right and keep right past a grass triangle and a telephone box. At the corner of the triangle cross a lane (70m) and continue along a track by South View. Continue past farm buildings and follow a track through a gap in a hedge and along the right-hand edge of a field. Continue under power lines (950m) and where the track turns right (150m) keep straight on N towards a stile at the edge of a wood (380m).

8. Enter the wood, which is part of the **Queen Elisabeth Country Park**, turn right and follow a path round to the left. Continue round another bend to the left, where a path crosses (450m). Continue N, above a hanger on the right, following Staunton Way signs, until another track crosses and the Staunton Way turns sharply back to the left (800m).

9. From this point, Hangers Way waymarks can be followed back to the start. Continue uphill above the hanger and then down along an obvious track. Look out for a *Hangers Way* sign (this is about 90m before the right fork at the *South Downs Way Walkers* sign on the outward route) (1,000m). Take a path on the right and follow it down through the hanger. Continue along the top of a field (200m) and across another to the car park (500m).

En route

Butser Ancient Farm: a serious research project as well as a fascinating glimpse into the Iron Age – buildings and agricultural methods have been re-created. Open daily, but ring to confirm Oct-Dec; tel: 01705 598838. Allow about an hour for a visit. *Caution:* the old site in Hillhampton Bottom to the north may still be shown on the map.

Chalton Windmill: a tower mill, has been converted to a residence and is not open to the public.

Finchdean: the inn is THE GEORGE (tel: 01705 412257).

Thatched cottage at Finchdean

Walk 4

Compton Down, Old Idsworth, Chalton (L), Sunwood Farm

Distances: out 10.5 km, 6.5 miles; return 9.0 km, 5.5 miles

Ascent: out 225m; return 230m

Times: out 2:45; return 2:30

Maps: Explorer 120, Landranger 197

Parking: limited space on the west side of the B2146 south of South Harting, where the SDW crosses (m/r 782184).

The walk: a mixture of woodland, downland and farmland. The outward route visits a fine yew wood and a beautifully situated chapel. The return passes some fine hangers on the escarpment.

Shorter walk: from Chalton, follow the lane past the by-way (see 7 below), take a path to Woodcroft Farm, and follow the Sussex Border Path to its junction with the SDW.

---

1. From the B2146 go NW along a track, the SDW. Just before a strip of woodland (600m), take a stile on the left. Turn right and left (15m), and follow a path through the wood. Continue into a field (630m) and follow its edge round to the right into woodland (450m). Turn left along a path, join a track (50m) and follow it along the lower edge of the wood. At the top of a rise cross a track (450m) and continue along a path. By a field on the left (350m) bear right along a path and continue S, between tall hedges and fields, to **Hucksholt Farm** (850m).

2. Turn right along a metalled track, with a barn on the left (which may not appear on the map). Just before the track bends right, take a path on the left (600m) along the edge of a field. Continue through a narrow strip of woodland (230m) and bear slightly left across the next field. Cross a lane (400m) and continue across a field to its left-hand corner and another lane (140m).

3. Turn right and follow the lane uphill to a metal gate on the left (100m) Follow a path beside the lane, and turn left before the edge of the field (80m). Continue uphill and turn right through a gate (90m). Follow a very faint path, bearing slightly uphill to the corner of **Robin Wood** (200m). Follow a track below the wood and then into it (200m). Go gently uphill and just before the top bear right along a track (250m).

Walk 4

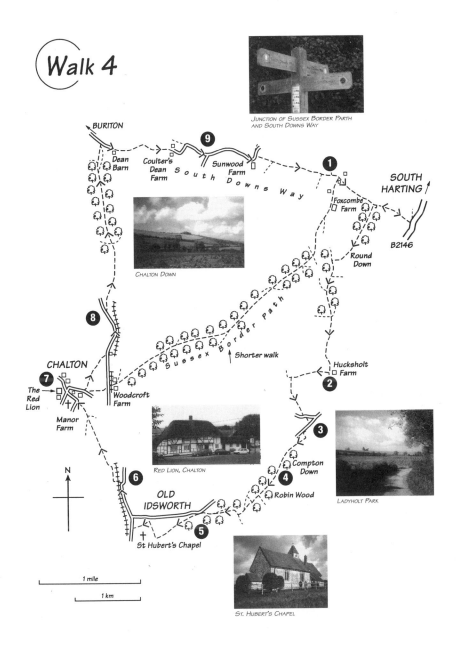

JUNCTION OF SUSSEX BORDER PARTH AND SOUTH DOWNS WAY

BURITON

Dean Barn

Coulter's Dean Farm

Sunwood Farm

South Downs Way

9

1

SOUTH HARTING

Foxcombe Farm

B2146

Round Down

CHALTON DOWN

Sussex Border Path

↑ Shorter walk

8

Hucksholt Farm

2

CHALTON

The Red Lion

7

Woodcroft Farm

Manor Farm

3

Compton Down

4

Robin Wood

LADYHOLT PARK

RED LION, CHALTON

6

OLD IDSWORTH

5

St Hubert's Chapel

N

1 mile

1 km

ST. HUBERT'S CHAPEL

4. For the next 750m keep just below the crest of the ridge, going SW. Go under power lines (600m), continue to the edge of the wood (150m) and turn right downhill. By the corner of a field (100m), follow a path round to the left and make a descending traverse. Join a track (300m) and where it swings left (100m) take a path on the right, which is not too obvious. Descend between fields towards a lane.

5. Just before the lane turn left (130m) and follow a path along the edge of a field. Continue along the edge of the next field and follow its edge round to the right (800m) (this RoW may not be shown on the map). Continue past *St Hubert's Chapel* at **Old Idsworth**, and take a path on the left (250m). Follow it past the chapel to a road (250m), turn right and continue past a lane on the right (160m).

6. Where the road bends right (450m), take a path on the left and follow it under the railway (60m). Continue across a field to a stile (90m), turn right and follow a path along an uncultivated strip of land. At its end, take a stile on the left (200m), go uphill beside a field (45m), turn right and follow a path above it. Where the fence bends, bear left uphill (150m) between scrub and continue WNW over a stile to the crest of the ridge (650m). Continue downhill, aiming for a yellow marker, and go through a field to the church at **Chalton**. Go through the graveyard to the inn (450m).

7. **Return:** turn left outside the inn and go the right of a grassy triangle and a telephone kiosk. Turn right along a lane (70m) and continue past Manor Farm. Just past the buildings take a track on the left, signed *Byway* (200m). Follow the track NE to a lane (650m) and turn left. Follow the lane, which runs near the railway and then swings away.

8. Take a stile on the right (650m) and follow a path through a field, towards and then under power lines (600m), and gently round to the left into a wood (350m). Cross a track (80m) and continue WNW along a track going steadily uphill. The going becomes level; continue past a track going off to the right (1,200m) and shortly take a path on the right (40m) as the track swings left. Follow the path downhill to a lane (350m) and turn right. This is the SDW, which is followed eastwards back to the start Just past cottages (200m) the lane becomes a track. Follow it uphill and down until it becomes a metalled lane again by **Coulter's Dean Farm** (950m).

The South Downs Way near Sunwood Farm

9. Continue past the private road (600m) to Ditcham Park School, where the spot height on the Explorer map should surely be 164m, to **Sunwood Farm** (700m). Follow the lane round to the left and, just past the last building, turn right (50m) along a track. The first high point (200m) is on the West Sussex border, where the SDW used to end abruptly before it was extended into Hampshire. Continue over a crossing track (1,100m) and join the outward route just past a barn (700m). Follow the track back to the start (600m).

En route

St Hubert's Chapel: stands in the middle of a field. It has mediaeval wall paintings, the discovery of which caused it to be re-named from St Peter's.

Chalton: THE RED LION is reputed to be the oldest inn in Hampshire, first built to house workmen re-building the CHURCH OF ST MICHAEL across the road. The menu gives its history. Opposite the inn is THE PRIORY, once the rectory, which is partly mediaeval.

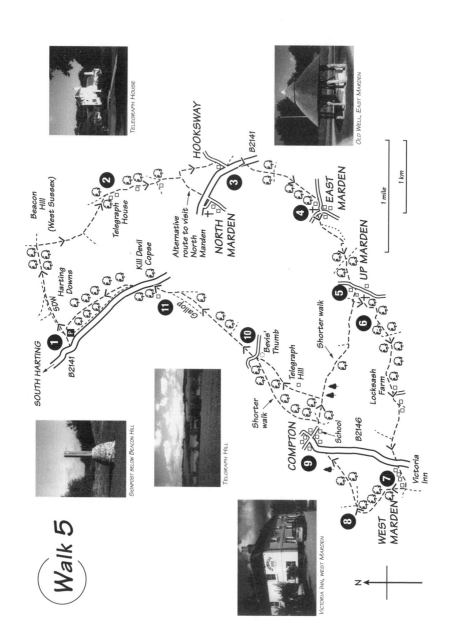

Walk 5

TELEGRAPH HOUSE

OLD WELL, EAST MARDEN

SIGNPOST BELOW BEACON HILL

TELEGRAPH HILL

VICTORIA INN, WEST MARDEN

1 mile
1 km

SOUTH HARTING

Beacon
Hill
(West Sussex)

SDW
Harting
Downs

Kill Devil
Copse

Telegraph
House

HOOKSWAY

B2141

Alternative
route to visit
North
Marden

NORTH
MARDEN

EAST
MARDEN

UP MARDEN

Gallop

Bevis'
Thumb

Telegraph
Hill

Shorter
walk

Shorter walk

Lockgash
Farm

Shorter
walk

COMPTON

School

B2146

Victoria
Inn

WEST
MARDEN

N

Walk 5

East Marden, Up Marden, West Marden (L), Compton

Distances: out 10.0 km, 6.5 miles; return 7.0 km, 4.5 miles

Ascent: out 220m; return 210m

Times: out 2:40; return 2:00

Maps: Explorer 120, Landranger 197

Parking: Harting Down on B2141 south of South Harting (m/r 790180)

The walk: visits three of the four Mardens. The fourth, North Marden, may be included by the detour shown on the map, at the cost of extra road walking.

Shorter walk: from Up Marden, continue along the track to Compton and lunch there.

---

1. From the car park turn right and go ENE along the SDW, following one of two parallel paths. Ascend a rise and descend to a dip (800m). Go over another rise and keep left to descend through scrub to another dip below **Beacon Hill** (the West Sussex one) (600m), where a signpost is mounted in a flint cairn. Turn right along a path which climbs the west flank of Beacon Hill (the summit is visited in Walk 7). Continue along a track joining from the left (1,200m) and then along a metalled drive past **Telegraph House** (200m).

2. Follow the drive ESE through gentle curves under a fine avenue of beeches until it swings sharply right (550m) just before a bungalow, and keep straight on through a small wooden gate (not the large one on the right). Follow a path between fields and continue along a track (120m). Follow this round to the left (250m) (turn right here to visit North Marden) and then to the right to a lane (600m), and turn right. Continue to the B2141 (170m) and turn left.

3. Cross a stile on the right (220m), and follow a faint path across the corner of a field. Bear left downhill across the middle of the next field, cross a strip of woodland (450m) and continue across the next field aiming just left of a row of trees. Continue with these on the right and, where they end, cross the corner of another field to a lane and turn right into *East Marden* (750m).

4. By the old well (150m), take the right-hand lane NW. Opposite a white cottage (70m), take a stile on the left. Cross a pathless field to its far corner (200m) and bear left along the edge of another field to-

The old well and church, East Marden

wards a wooded hillside. Follow the edge of the field round to the right (350m) to a stile on the left (70m). Continue along the edge of a field into a wood (180m) and follow a path steeply uphill over a crossing path. Continue along the edge of a field to a lane (380m), and turn left into *Up Marden*.

Take a track on the right (120m) signed *Up Marden Church*; the church can be visited by a path on the left. Go a little way downhill, cross a stile on the left (200m) at the corner of a field and continue beside a row of trees. At a corner turn right (170m), and continue along the edge of the next field with woodland on the left. Follow the edge of the field round to the left and then to the right (160m). Go down into a dip and part way up the other side. Turn left into a wood (200m) and immediately bear right along a track.

6. Continue past a track on the left (50m), go downhill and take a path on the right (400m). Cross a field to a white disc (240m), bear left at a stile (40m) and follow a path uphill through woodland. Join a track (90m) and continue past the buildings of Locksash Farm (labelled thus on the OS map; the house a little further along the lane also bears this name) to a lane (200m). Keep right and follow the lane W to cross the B2146 (950m) into *West Marden*, and continue to the inn (60m).

7. **Return:** from the inn, turn right and walk through the village. Where

the road bends left (250m) two RoWs go off to the right. Take the first, lower one beside a house, Marden Down. Start along the drive, then follow a path on the left N through woodland. Go along the hillside and into a field (500m). Continue along its bottom with a wood on the right. Continue along the bottom of another field, and in the next, just before a corner (350m), turn right by a pond.

8. Follow a track up a short rise. At the top (90m) two RoWs go off to the left. Take the right-hand one, a faint path, and follow it ENE away from the track, as the church at Compton comes into view. Continue over a stile and through a kissing gate (270m), then through woodland to another kissing gate (180m). Bear left across a field to the middle of its left-hand side. Continue though a row of pines (240m) and across a field to the B2146 (170m). Turn left into *Compton*.

9. Just past the Coach and Horses turn right (150m), take the right-hand of two roads and follow it past the school (120m), where a path on the left leads to St Mary's Church. The next section can be confusing –the objective is to go E, almost straight up the hill ahead. Follow the path uphill. At a junction of paths (120m) bear left, ignoring paths on either side. Take a narrow path on the right (40m) which goes steeply uphill through woodland (the ascent of **Telegraph Hill** can be avoided by keeping straight on at this point). At a stile (50m), continue uphill along the edge of two fields. Just before woodland at the top, (300m) turn left and then keep left at a junction of tracks. Continue NNE along the ridge past a house on the hilltop (320m) and continue downhill along its drive. Uppark is well seen on the left. Just before a lane (800m) *Bevis's Thumb* can be seen on the right.

10. Cross the lane and follow a track NE along the edge of a field. Continue past a wood on the right and along the edge of another field. At a kink in the path, where power lines make a right angle, (1,000m) move to the right and continue with a fenced gallop on the left. At the corner of the field (260m) bear left along a path with woodland on the left and a field on the right. By a house with a tall arched gate (250m) follow the path round to the right, join a track and follow it to the B2141 (250m).

11. Just before the road turn left along a path. Cross the road (50m) to a footpath, continue through a strip of woodland to a field at **Kill**

Devil Copse and turn left (25m). Follow a path parallel to the road into a wood (200m) and turn right through a kissing gate. Take the left of two paths and follow it to a junction (100m). From this point the shortest way back to the car park is to take a kissing gate on the left and follow a path through the wood. However, it is more pleasant to follow a grassy path over downland with the wood on the left. Go gently uphill and continue NW to the SDW (1,000m) and turn left back to the car park.

En route

East Marden: the attractions of the little village include flint buildings and ST PETER'S CHURCH. The covered OLD WELL was the village's only source of drinking water until 1924.

Up Marden: (sometimes Upmarden), high on the downs, is tiny. Nairn and Pevsner state that the simple CHURCH OF ST MICHAEL is "one of the loveliest in England". The original chancel arch is supported by a later one built inside it.

West Marden: the largest of the four. There are some attractive flint houses, but the village has lost its church. The inn is THE VICTORIA INN (tel: 01705 631722).

Compton: has the COACH AND HORSES and a village store.

Bevis's Thumb: the largest long barrow in West Sussex.

Walk 6

West Dean, Chilgrove, Kingley Vale, Stoughton (L)

Distances: out 11.0 km, 7.0 miles; return 9.5 km, 6.0 miles

Ascent: out 285m; return 235m

Times: out 2:55; return 2:35

Maps: Explorer 120, Landranger 197

Parking: in lanes behind the Selsey Arms (m/r 857124)

The walk: the highlight is Kingley Vale, the finest yew forest in Europe, and the walk has been designed to visit as much of it as possible. Bow Hill is a fine viewpoint.

Shorter walk: On the outward route, the descent into and the climb from Yew Tree Grove can be avoided by the route shown on the map. On the return route, initially follow the outward route from Stoughton.

---

1. The **Selsey Arms** is assumed to be the starting point. From the inn, walk NE along the A286. Opposite a lane, take a track on the left (220m) and then, by the corner of a wood (120m), take a path on the left. Continue along the edge of the wood into a field (300m) and at a fence (160m) turn left to a lane (100m). Turn right and take a track on the left (15m) uphill through a wood, **Whitedown Plantation**. A track joins from the right. At the top (600m), continue WNW along the edge of a field past **Lodge Hill Farm**.

2. Continue past a barn (which may not be shown on the map) and across two fields. Cross the next field and follow its edge for a short distance, then cross a stile and continue along a track (650m) to a T-junction (320m). Continue along a lane over crossroads (850m) and bear left to the B2141 (100m).

3. Turn right and follow the road round to the left. A little before The White Horse at **Chilgrove**, turn sharply back left along a track (400m), and follow it uphill into woodland. At the top (600m) turn left, and continue S along the ridge to a sign *Kingley Vale National Nature Reserve* (700m). Just past **Blackbush House** (500m), follow the track round a slight zigzag, and continue along the ridge. Where two tracks run side by side, take the one on the left and continue over crossing tracks. By a fence on the left (1,100m) keep right along the more distinct track. Continue over a crossing track; just past

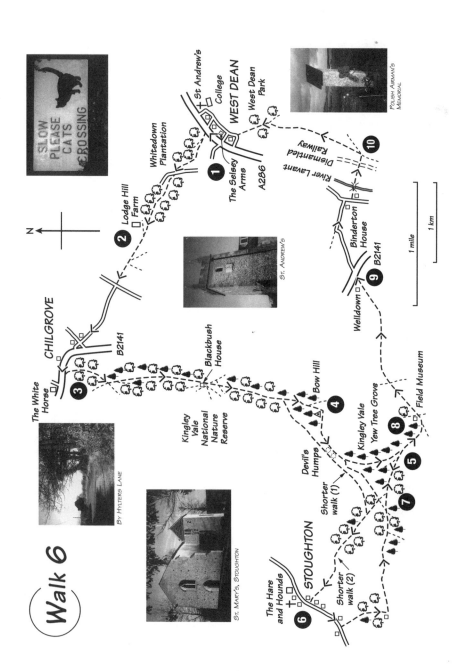

Walk 6

SLOW
PLEASE
CATS
CROSSING

St Andrew's
College
WEST DEAN
West Dean Park

POLISH AIRMAN'S
MEMORIAL

Whitedown Plantation

Lodge Hill Farm

The Selsey Arms
A286

1

2

N

ST. ANDREW'S

River Lavant
Dismantled Railway

10

Binderton House
B2141

Welldown

9

CHILGROVE
B2141

The White Horse

3

Blackbush House

Bow Hill

4

8

Field Museum

5

BY HYLTERS LANE

Kingley Vale National Nature Reserve

Kingley Vale
Yew Tree Grove

Devil's Humps

Shorter walk (1)

7

STOUGHTON

Shorter walk (2)

The Hare and Hounds

6

ST. MARY'S, STOUGHTON

1 mile
1 km

here the triangulation pillar on **Bow Hill** lies off the main track on the right (200m).

4. Follow the track round to the right and onto open ground (400m), where there are excellent views and barrows known as **The Devil's Humps**. At the end of the open ground (300m), where two tracks run side by side, take the one on the left and go gently downhill and round to the left through Yew Tree Grove in *Kingley Vale*.

5. Where a field appears on the right, turn sharply back to the right (800m) and follow a track running NW along the edge of the forest. Keep left at a fork and continue beside the forest. Go under an arch of yews and fork right (450m). Continue uphill to a field (part of which may be shown as woodland on the map) and keep right along its edge. Go over the brow of a hill and down into woodland (550m), where a track is joined. Continue into fields (380m), past a memorial to a Polish airman. Continue to a lane (800m) and turn right into *Stoughton* and the inn (300m).

6. **Return:** walk back along the lane, past the point where it was joined, to a row of houses. Just past the last one (800m) take a path on the left along the edge of a field. Go uphill into a wood (350m) and follow a path steeply uphill. Join another path near the top, continue over a track, and join a path at the corner of a field. Turn left and continue to ruined buildings on the ridge (280m). Turn left and follow a track E along the ridge into woodland (850m). Continue to a field on the left (400m) (which may be partly shown as woodland on the map).

7. About 60m before the corner of the field, take a path on the right. Join the outward route by the arch of yews (350m) and continue gently downhill, soon with fields on the right. Continue past the point where the path was joined on the outward route (450m) by Yew Tree Grove. At the bottom of the hill turn left at a T-junction (500m).

8. A distinctive carving on the left marks the position of the Field Museum (150m). Continue NE along the track past the edge of the forest (150m) and between fields (in 1999, plans were afoot to convert the land to the south into a golf course). Go over a crossing track (350m) with The Trundle prominent ahead. Continue to the B2141 by **Welldown** and turn right (1,400m).

9. Turn left (45m) along a lane. At a bend to the right (550m) look back

Lane near Welldown

for a fine view of Kingley Vale. Continue to the A286 (400m) by **Binderton House**, cross and turn right. Take a track on the left (70m) just before houses. Continue ESE along a path, cross the **River Lavant** by a footbridge, and go over the old railway to a gate (600m).

10. Turn left, and follow a path NNE along the bottom edge of a field (not the path going diagonally uphill). Continue along the lower edges of fields to the imposing flint wall which encloses West Dean Park (1,250m) and turn left along a track. Follow this to the bridge over the river at **West Dean** and walk back to the start (650m).

En route

West Dean: not to be confused with Westdean in East Sussex, lies in the valley of the infant RIVER LAVANT. It contains the CHURCH OF ST ANDREW and WEST DEAN COLLEGE (not open to the public). Most of the buildings lie on narrow lanes just east of the A286. WEST DEAN GARDENS are open Mar – Oct, daily; tel: 01243 818210.

Kingley Vale: legend has it that the magnificent yews are descended from those planted on the graves of fallen warriors. The FIELD MUSEUM can be visited on the return.

Stoughton: ST MARY'S CHURCH is Saxon, and its belfry has Quarr stones from the Isle of Wight. There is a splendid show of daffodils in Spring. The inn is the HARE AND HOUNDS (tel: 01705 631433).

Walk 7

Linch Down, Beacon Hill (W Sussex), Hooksway (L)

Distances: out 11.0 km, 6.5 miles; return 8.0 km, 5.0 miles

Ascent: out 285m; return 195m

Times: out 2:55; return 2:05

Maps: Explorer 120, Landranger 197

Parking: car park on the west side of the A286, where the SDW crosses (m/r 875166). This can be difficult to spot from the road – look out for SDW signs and a bus stop.

The walk: the outward route follows a fine section of the SDW and visits Beacon Hill, one of the best summits. The return is a pleasant mixture of woodland and downland. Binoculars may be useful in Monkton Wood (see para. 1).

Shorter walks: 1. On the outward route, keep straight on to Hooksway from The Devil's Jumps (which many walkers do by mistake anyway). 2. On the return route, use the same track and then follow the SDW back to the start.

Caution: the Royal Oak is closed on Mondays.

---

1. From the car park, follow a track, the SDW, W past the oddly named Hilltop (200m) and up onto **Cocking Down**. A track crosses at the top of the hill (1,800). Continue past the triangulation pillar (850m) on **Linch Down**, where Beacon Hill appears on the horizon. Cross **Didling Hill** and enter **Monkton Wood**, (1,400m), where exotic birds and animals may be seen and heard. Follow the track round to the left (400m). Just past a field a row of barrows known as **The Devil's Jumps** may be seen on the right (450m), and visited by means of a path.

2. A little past here, on **Philliswood Down**, is a spot where many walkers go astray. At a crossing track (300m) turn right (NW) – the usual error is to go straight on. After about 100m look out for a memorial to a German airman on the right. Follow the track downhill and right and left into open country.

3. Turn left at a T-junction (1,100m) towards **Buriton Farm,** and then right (30m) along a path. Follow the path into woodland (250m) and keep left along its edge. Continue along the lower edge of a field (150m), above a track which joins from the right. In the next field (250m), follow the path round to the left along its edge and then bear

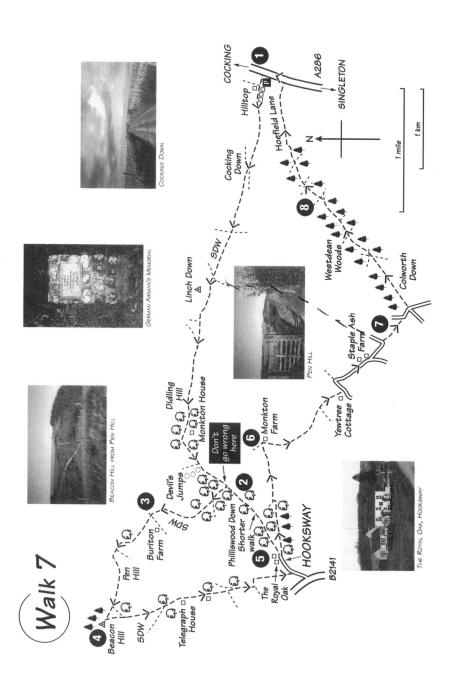

COCKING

SINGLETON

A286

Hilltop

Hoefield Lane

Cocking Down

Cocking Down

SDW

N

1 mile

1 km

Linch Down

German Airman's Memorial

Didling Hill

Monkton House

Don't go wrong here

Monkton Farm

Westdean Woods

Colworth Down

Staple Ash Farm

Pen Hill

Yewtree Cottage

Devil's Jumps

Philliswood Down

Shorter walk

HOOKSWAY

Beacon Hill from Pen Hill

Buriton Farm

SDW

Pen Hill

The Royal Oak

B2141

The Royal Oak, Hooksway

Walk 7

Beacon Hill

SDW

Telegraph House

right up **Pen Hill**
(450m). From the
summit go down to
a dip (250m), where
the SDW goes off to
the left (and may be
followed to by-pass
the ascent). Ascend
the steep slope (zig-
zagging helps) to
the summit of *Bea-
con Hill* (250m).

4. Reverse the first
part of the ascent,
then bear right be-
low cultivated
ground to re-join a
the SDW (200m).
Go ESE along the
flank of the hill into
woodland and,
where the SDW
swings back north,
bear left (600m) and
continue along a
metalled drive past

Beacon Hill from Pen Hill

Telegraph House (200m). Follow the drive through gentle curves
under a fine avenue of beeches until it swings sharply right (550m)
just before a bungalow, and keep straight on through a small
wooden gate (not the large one on the right). Follow a path between
fields and continue along a track (120m). Follow this round to the
left (250m), and then to the right, to a lane (600m), and turn left into
Hooksway (250m).

5. **Return:** there are four RoWs just north of the inn, so care is needed.
Turn left and walk to a junction of three tracks just past the restaurant (30m). Take the one on the right, and almost immediately cross
a stile on the left (10m) and follow a path into woodland. Go uphill
and continue ENE over a ride and two crossing tracks. A track joins
from the right (650m); almost immediately turn right along a cross-

ing track. Take a path on the left (60m), cross a track (15m), and continue uphill. Go through a kissing gate and along the edge of a field. Continue along the edge of the next field over the crest of a ridge. In the next go downhill towards a flint building, named on the map as **Monkton Farm** (700m).

6. Just before the building, turn right and follow a grassy track uphill. Continue S and then SE through and beside a long strip of woodland to a lane by **Yewtree Cottage**. (1,300m). Turn left and follow the lane round a right-hand bend. Just past **Staple Ash Farm** (700m) fork left and follow a lane until it bends sharply left (250m).

7. Keep straight on (SE) along a track, over a rise and down into a wood. Continue along a lane (400m) and opposite a lane on the right (120m) take a track on the left, which runs in a straight line with fields on the right and woodland on the left. Continue over **Colworth Down** into **Westdean Woods** (800m) and, at a junction of tracks, keep straight on. The numerous tracks in this wood can be confusing – remember that the route goes consistently NE. Copious *Private* signs also reduce the chances of error.

8. Follow the track uphill. At the top (1,000m) bear left at a Y-junction, cross a prominent track and continue NE. At a fork (60m), keep right. Follow the track over a crossing track (150m), and then to the right and downhill to a field on the left (400m). At the corner of the field turn left and then right (30m) along a track (**Hoefield Lane**) between tall hedges. Continue down to the A286 (800m) and tun left back to the start (300m).

En route

Beacon Hill: has a triangulation pillar, and fine views in all directions except NE, where trees have been planted. The view indicator does not recognise this problem, and has a distinct bias in favour of NT properties.

Hooksway: The inn is THE ROYAL OAK (tel: 01243 535527; closed on Mondays) – don't miss the cuttings about the former landlord. There is also THE HIDEAWAY restaurant (tel: 01243 535372).

Walk 8

Levin Down, The Trundle, Singleton (L)

Distances: out 12.5 km, 8.0 miles; return 7.0 km, 4.5 miles

Ascent: out 325m; return 210m

Times: out 3:25; return 2:00

Maps: Explorer 120, Landranger 197

Parking: (as Walk 7) car park on the west side of the A286 above Cocking, where the SDW crosses. (m/r 875166). This can be difficult to spot from the road – look out for SDW signs and a bus stop.

The walk: the highlights are Levin Down, where the famous turf is conserved, and the hill fort of The Trundle. A long outward walk is balanced by a short return.

Shorter Walks: 1. From Charlton, follow a lane to The Trundle. **2.** From this lane take a path direct to Singleton. **3.** In Westdean Woods, follow Walk 7 back to the start (see para. 10).

Caution: avoid Goodwood race days.

---

1. Cross the road and follow a track (the SDW) E onto **Manorfarm Down**. Just before some trees, turn right (1,800m) and follow a track downhill through woodland. Turn right along a crossing track (180m), continue downhill and bear left at a junction (450m). There is now a long, straight downhill trudge almost exactly due south. At the bottom (1,000m) keep straight on at a junction and continue between fields.

2. Pass a path to **Broadham House** on the right (100m) and go gently uphill to a junction of tracks (350m) at the top. Bear round to the left and, just past a pit, go up steps on the right (50m) onto *Levin Down*. Continue along the edge of a field with woodland on the left. Just before a group of trees in the field, take a path on the left (300m) and follow it through the wood. Continue along the flank of the hill, as The Trundle and the stands of the race course appear ahead. Follow the path downhill to a fence (800m) and continue beside it. Cross two stiles (100m) and bear left to a road (200m).

3. Turn left into *Charlton*. Continue through the centre of the village and, just past the Fox, take a lane on the right (250m). Follow it round to the right (120m) and turn left at a T-junction. Pass a memorial to the men of The Sussex Yeomanry, and continue along a track between attractive old houses, the last of which, on the left, is Fox Hall. Follow the track uphill into woodland. **Goodwood Racecourse** appears on the right – this would seem to be a good place for a free view. Continue to a road (1,900m) and cross into **Good wood Country Park**.

4. Walk away from the road and turn right (60m). Follow a path WSW along a winding course roughly parallel to the road, of which there are only glimpses. The path is waymarked *Goodwood Country Park Circular Walk 1*. By **Harroway's Car Park** (950m) turn left along a track and very shortly (55m) climb up to open ground on the right and a metalled track by a camp site (60m). Turn left and, where the track divides (180m), turn right along the edge of the campsite, keeping wooden railings on the right. Go over the crest of the hill and down into woodland (150m). Turn right along a path and continue along a road.

5. Just before the stands, turn left along a road (250m), follow it downhill and round to the right, and turn right at a junction (380m). Opposite the stands, turn left onto an old section of road (320m), then take a path on the left (70m) and pass a small brick building. Go steeply uphill, then turn right and left to follow a path beside iron railings. Take a kissing gate on the right (200m) and bear left uphill to the summit of *The Trundle* (120).

6. Go downhill to the right of the right-hand of the two masts, following a grassy path through a gap in the ramparts. Bear left down to the **Triangle Car Park** (350m). Cross a road and go N along a lane signposted *Charlton*. At a passing space, take a path on the left (550m) and follow waymark posts diagonally across a field. Continue along the top of a field (400m), and follow a track down into *Singleton* (800m). Follow a path through the churchyard, turn left and then right along a lane and continue to the inn (100m).

7. **Return:** from the inn, turn right and walk W to the A286 (160m). The *Open Air Museum* is a little further along the A286. Turn right beside the Post Office, follow a track over a bridge, and continue along the edge of a cricket ground. Behind the pavilion, formerly a barn, cross a stile (120m) and follow the edge of a field round to the right. Cross a footbridge and a stile on the left, where there is a NT sign *Drovers Estate*, and follow a path uphill between fences and hedges.

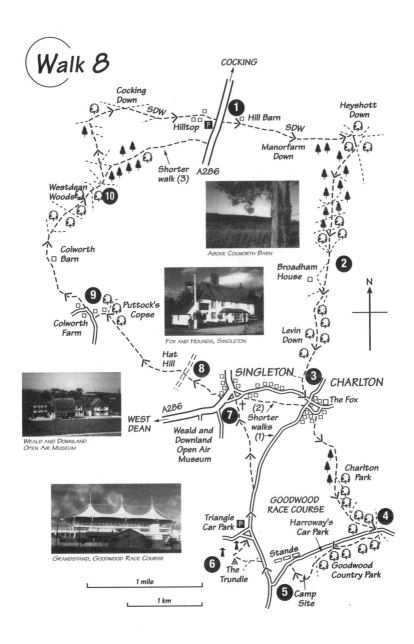

Walk 8

COCKING

Cocking Down

SDW

Hilltop

Hill Barn

SDW

Heyshott Down

Manorfarm Down

Shorter walk (3)

A286

Westdean Woods

10

Colworth Barn

ABOVE COLWORTH BARN

Broadham House

N

9

Puttock's Copse

Colworth Farm

FOX AND HOUNDS, SINGLETON

Levin Down

Hat Hill

8

SINGLETON

3

CHARLTON

The Fox

WEALD AND DOWNLAND OPEN AIR MUSEUM

WEST DEAN

A286

Weald and Downland Open Air Museum

7

(2) Shorter walks (1)

Charlton Park

GOODWOOD RACE COURSE

GRANDSTAND, GOODWOOD RACE COURSE

Triangle Car Park

Harroway's Car Park

Stands

4

Goodwood Country Park

6

The Trundle

5

Camp Site

1 mile

1 km

The village pond at Singleton

8. Cross a disused railway (450m) and continue up **Hat Hill**, bearing round to the left above woodland. Continue along the edge of a field, passing under power lines. Follow the edges of two more fields NW, going under the power lines again. At the corner of the second field (1,100m) cross a stile on the left and continue with woodland on the right. Follow the edge of the next field and at its corner turn left along a track (300m), past an old corrugated iron building. Continue to a lane and turn right (200m).

9. At **Colworth Farm**, where the lane ends (150m), continue along a track and follow it downhill to lonely **Colworth Barn** (850m). Follow the track uphill into **Westdean Woods** and, at a junction (350m), take the right-hand track. The chances of going wrong in this wood are minimised by *Private* signs.

10. Follow the track NE and uphill. At the top (1,000m), bear left at a Y-junction, cross a prominent track and continue NE. At a fork (60m), keep left (the right fork followed in Walk 7 offers a shorter way back to the start). Continue NNW uphill to the edge of the forest, and turn right at a T-junction (800m). Go downhill, ENE, through forest and between fields to a track, the SDW, at **Cocking Down** (550m). Turn right and walk back to the start (1,200m).

En route

Levin Down: contains one of the best examples of downland turf. This is due to the work of the SUSSEX WILDLIFE TRUST, which manages the central part, and has partly cleared the ground to restore the grazing.

Charlton: The full name of the inn is THE FOX GOES FREE. The WOODSTOCK HOUSE HOTEL is open to non-residents. FOX HALL was once a hunting lodge owned by the Duke of Richmond. It has recently been restored by the Landmark Trust.

The Trundle: ST ROCHE'S HILL is the correct term, but the name of the Iron Age fort on its summit is usually preferred. It is a fine viewpoint, marred by radio towers and the proximity of roads, car parks and buildings. The Isle of Purbeck is well seen. There is a triangulation pillar and a barrow, surrounded by the ramparts of the fort.

Singleton: features on the 1998 Explorer map. The CHURCH OF THE BLESSED VIRGIN MARY has a Saxon tower. The only inn now is THE FOX AND HOUNDS (tel: 01243 811251) The Horse and Groom has closed, as has the village store. There is also the STUDIO TEA ROOM (tel: 01243 811899).

The Weald and Downland Open Air Museum: has over 40 historic buildings, rescued and rebuilt. There are also Southdown sheep, Sussex cattle, a restaurant and picnic facilities. A visit is strongly recommended, but a half day should be allowed at least, more than can be combined with this walk. Open March – October daily; November – February Wed, Sat, Sun; tel: 01243 811348.

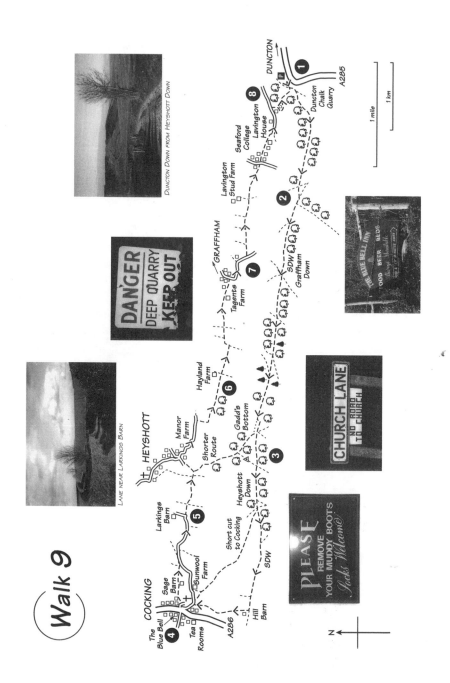

DUNCTON DOWN FROM HEYSHOTT DOWN

LANE NEAR LARKINGS BARN

Walk 9

DANGER DEEP QUARRY KEEP OUT

THE BLUE BELL INN · FOOD · BEER · BEDS

CHURCH LANE NO ROAD TO GRAFFHAM

PLEASE REMOVE YOUR MUDDY BOOTS Socks Welcome!

DUNCTON
A285
Duncton Chalk Quarry
Lavington House
Seaford College
Lavington Stud Farm
GRAFFHAM
SDW
Graffham Down
Tagents Farm
Hayland Farm
Gadd's Bottom
Manor Farm
Shorter Route
HEYSHOTT
Larkings Barn
Sunwool Farm
Sage Barn
COCKING
The Blue Bell
Tea Rooms
A286
Hill Barn
SDW
Short cut to Cocking
Heyshott Down

N

1 mile
1 km

Walk 9

Graffham Down, Heyshott Down, Cocking (L),

Distances: out 8.5 km, 5.5 miles; return 9.0 km, 5.5 miles

Ascent: out 135m; return 190m

Times: out 2:10; return 2:20

Maps: Explorer 120, 121, Landranger 197

Parking: car park at Duncton Hill Viewpoint, halfway up the hill on A285 (m/r 954160).

The walk: views from the ridge are limited by woodland. The return section takes advantage of the absence of the usual "underhill" lane to explore the foot of the escarpment. Compass directions are not really needed – the outward route goes almost entirely due west, and the return due east.

Shorter walk: just past the kink in the SDW above Gadd's Bottom (m/r 905165, see route description), follow the path down to Heyshott and turn left along the lane to The Unicorn Inn. The map will probably show the path starting *from* the zigzag, but this route is not followed on the ground.

---

1. From the car park, take a path uphill beside the road. Turn left at a T-junction (75m) and keep left at a fork (45m). Follow the path round to the right away from the road and uphill with **Duncton Chalk Quarry** on the left. Continue uphill though woodland, and then between fields (950m) (the map may show woodland on the left where there are now fields). By a small wood on the right there is a junction of paths (550m). Keep straight on,and cross a field diagonally; the state of the path varies with ploughing and crops. Continue to a track (150m) (the SDW) and turn right.

2. Continue along the crest of the ridge. At **Graffham Down** (1,150m), the track enters woodland. Continue, as a bridleway joins from the left, into more open country (1,700m). The zigzag above **Gadd's Bottom** (450m) occurs just over 100m to the east of the position shown on the map. Continue to a path on the right (600m), which leads to the triangulation pillar on **Heyshott Down**, a good viewpoint.

3. Continue to a strip of woodland (500m). Just through it (90m), a path on the right offers a shorter descent to Cocking. Continue along the SDW and join a made track just above Hill Barn. Pass between two cottages (1,500m) which wear the yellow livery of the Cowdray Estate, and turn right (N) along a track through the farm buildings.

Go downhill past an old chalk pit (450m) as the church at Cocking appears ahead. Turn left along a lane by the church (300m) and walk into **Cocking** (200m). Turn left along the A286 to the inn; the tea rooms are further along the road to the south.

4. **Return:** go E along **Mill Lane**, almost opposite the inn, until it bends right (80m). Continue along a track across a stream and round to the left. Take a narrow path by a garage and follow it right and left beside a garden. Just past the garden turn right and go up steps into a field (140m). Follow its edge round to the left to **Sage (Sages?) Barn** (160m), which is a private residence. Bear left across a yard and take a path across a field with the house on the right. Continue across a field to a stile (300m) and turn right and then left (15m) along a lane.

5. Where the lane turns left to **Larkins Barn** (750m) keep straight on along a track. Where another track joins (700m), follow it round to the left towards **Heyshott**. Just before a lane (250m), turn right along a private road signed *Manor Farm*. Follow this left, right and left between the farm buildings. Continue past a track on the right (420m) and take the next track on the right (220m) towards the foot of the escarpment. Go through a gate (170m) and follow the track round to the left. Continue along the foot of the escarpment and where the track swings right, continue across fields by **Hayland Farm** (750m).

6. Continue to a crossing path (450m), turn left and follow it round to the right. This section can be very muddy. Continue along a track to a large pink house (500m), where the RoW follows a track to the left of a private road. At **Tagents Farm** (250m) join the private road and continue to a lane at the southern outskirts of *Graffham* (300m). Turn right, and follow the lane past the church to its end (450m).

7. Turn left along the private road to **Seaford College**. Continue past Lavington Stud Farm (850m) and between the College buildings. Just past *Lavington House*, high on the right (1,000m), keep right at a fork. Walk to the end of a lane (50m) and turn left. Continue to a private house on the right, through whose grounds a river flows, and turn right along its gravel drive (400m).

8. Immediately past the house turn right up a grassy path and continue through a kissing gate into a wood. Just before a gate, (150m) turn left and follow a path steeply uphill (400m). At a fork keep left and go slightly downhill. Keep left (40m) beside the A285 and turn right (45m) back to the car park (75m).

En route

Cocking: has THE BLUE BELL INN, a Post Office/confectioners and THE MOONLIGHT COTTAGE TEA ROOMS (B&B, tel: 01730 813336). The dedication of the CHURCH is unknown. The MANOR FARMHOUSE opposite (not open to the public) used to be a Cluniac monastery.

Graffham: the village centre is a kilometre to the north of the walk, but some attractive flint buildings are passed, including the CHURCH OF ST GILES and the SCHOOL.

Cocking church

Lavington House: now part of SEAFORD COLLEGE, has associations with two XIX century churchmen, Bishop Wilberforce and Cardinal Manning. Behind the house is the little CHURCH OF ST PETER.

Walk 10

Upwaltham, East Dean, Halnaker (L), Stane Street

Distances: out 10.5 km, 6.5 miles; return 10.0 km, 6.0 miles

Ascent: out 205m; return 275m

Times: out 2:45; return 2:40

Maps: Explorer 121, Landranger 197

Parking: limited space where Droke Lane to East Dean leaves the A285 (m/r 940133)

The walk: there are long stretches of deciduous woodland, attractive in summer, even better in late autumn. The famous Halnaker Windmill is visited, and much of the return lies along Stane Street.

Shorter walk: from the parking place, follow Droke Lane to East Dean.

---

1. Walk NE along the A285 towards **Upwaltham**. Opposite the Old Toll House (150m), take a stile on the left, and go NW uphill along the edge of a field. Continue through a clump of trees and join a track (350m). Continue up **Heath Hill** and, as the gradient eases, bear round to the right above **Heath Hanger**. At the corner of the field (1,250m) cross a stile on the left into woodland and follow a short path to a crossing path (30m). Turn left, walk to a junction (750m) and continue WSW along a made track in a straight line to another junction (800m).

2. Turn left along another made track and where it swings left (120m) keep straight on along a grassy path. Continue SW to a field on the left at **High Down** (500m) and go downhill to a lane (1,100m). Turn right and, just before the first building on the left (160m), turn left into a field. To explore **East Dean** continue along the lane.

3. Follow a wooden fence and the edge of a field S to a sunken path (190m). Turn left and right (15m) and follow a path along the edge of a field. Continue along the edge of the next field up **Eastdean Hill** and follow the path into a wood (350m). Continue uphill past a path on the left (which the map show in the field). Continue over a crossing path (100m) and as the gradient eases join a track (80m) and bear left along it. At the top, where a track goes off to the right, bear left (250m). Continue SE until a path (which may not be shown as a RoW on the map) joins from the left (450m). Just past here (20m)

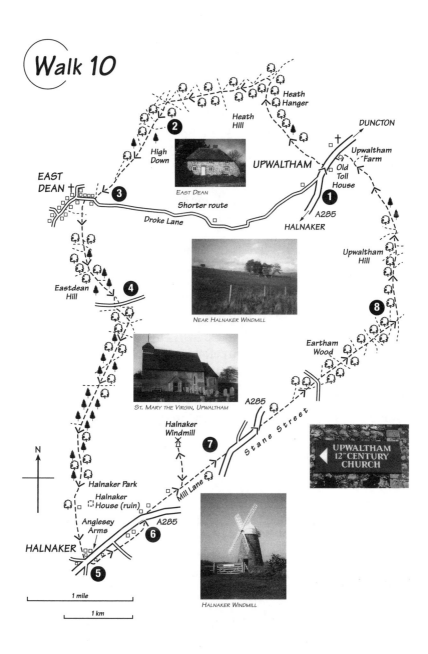

Walk 10

Heath Hanger

Heath Hill

DUNCTON

2

High Down

UPWALTHAM

Upwaltham Farm

EAST DEAN

3

EAST DEAN

Shorter route

Old Toll House

1

Droke Lane

A285

HALNAKER

Eastdean Hill

4

Upwaltham Hill

8

NEAR HALNAKER WINDMILL

Eartham Wood

ST. MARY THE VIRGIN, UPWALTHAM

A285

Stane Street

Halnaker Windmill

7

UPWALTHAM 12ᵀᴴ CENTURY CHURCH

N

Halnaker Park

Halnaker House (ruin)

Mill Lane

Anglesey Arms

A285

6

HALNAKER

5

1 mile

1 km

HALNAKER WINDMILL

take a path on the right, cross the corner of a field and continue across a road (130m).

4. Take a track (not the path on the left) and continue SE. Halnaker Windmill can be seen on the horizon. Just before a gate (300m) turn right and follow a track downhill through woodland. There is now a long, straight and slightly boring trudge SSW until a track crosses and a field appears on the right (1,650m). Follow the track S into open country with a flint wall on the right (850m). Soon, the ruins of old Halnaker House can be seen by looking back to the left, together with some massive dead trees. Continue along a lane to a road junction (1,000m) and turn left along the A285 to *Halnaker* and the inn (100m).

5. **Return:** walk back to the road junction (100m) and turn left down The Street. Pass a track on the left and take a path just past it along the edge of a field. At the corner of the field, where a path goes off right (150m), follow a left-right zigzag and continue NE along the edge of a field. Cross the field between an avenue of young trees to a private road (350m), and turn right and then left (60m) across a field. Cross another field, go down into a dip (350m), bear right and left (20m) and cross a field to a gap and the A285 (250m).

6. Cross and turn right along a track, **Mill Lane,** with a sign *Warehead Farm.* This is part of Stane Street, which is followed NE in almost a straight line for the next four-and-a-half kilometres. Keep right past Mill Cottage and follow the track uphill. At the end of the track (600m) there are two paths. To visit *Halnaker Windmill*, the top of which is visible, cross a stile just to the right of two metal gates and follow a path N to the windmill (550m).

7. As there is, unfortunately, only one RoW to the mill, return to the end of the track (550m), bear round to the left, climb a few steps (which are not obvious) and continue in the previous direction along Stane Street, now a narrow, winding path. At the corner of a wood (300m), move left into a field and continue with the wood on the right. Follow power lines across a field to the A285 (500m).

8. Follow the road until it swings left (480m). Keep straight on along a path which follows the course of **Stane Street** though woodland and fields, uphill and down, to a road (1,100m). Cross and continue along a path (not a made track which swings left). Continue along a track which follows a straight line through woodland. Just before

the top of a rise there is a junction of six RoWs, a large signpost, and a seat (1,450m).

9. Leave Stane Street by taking the second track on the left, signposted *Upwaltham*. There is now a long climb N through woodland over **Upwaltham Hill.** Just before the top there is a T-junction (1,200m). Turn right and left (30m) and keep right at a fork (60m). Continue along the edge of a field, and then follow a grassy track NW down past the corner of a wood to **Upwaltham Farm** (1,350m). Turn left along a metalled track, and follow it round to the right between the farm buildings to the A285 (100m). The church, well seen on the descent, can be visited by a short detour along the track opposite. Turn left back to the start (350m).

En route

East Dean: has many attractive flint buildings. Just past NEWHOUSE LANE on the right a path leads to the X11 century ALL SAINTS CHURCH. Further along the lane is THE HURDLEMAKERS INN. The name is a relic of a former village industry – hurdles were vital to the old farming method of confining sheep at night to fertilise arable fields.

All Saints Church, East Dean

Stane Street: the Roman road which linked London and Chichester. Much of the agger (the embankment carrying the road), and the ditches and banks on either side can be clearly seen.

Halnaker: (pronounced Hannaker) is a small village on a busy road. The inn is THE ANGLESEY ARMS. it is possible to enter the famous WINDMILL, but the brick tower is now an empty shell. Hilaire Belloc wrote a sad poem about it when it was a ruin; it has since been twice restored.

Upwaltham: the little CHURCH OF ST MARY THE VIRGIN is Saxon, and has been less altered than many. All the trees in the churchyard were blown down in 1987, and were replaced by gifts from local families.

Walk 11

Stane Street, Slindon (L), Great Down, Barlavington Down

Distances: out 11.0 km, 7.0 miles; return 9.5 km, miles 6.0

Ascent: out 235m; return 275m

Times: out 3:00; return 2:40

Maps: Explorer 121, Landranger 197

Parking: on the W side of the A285 at the entrance to Duncton Chalk Quarry (m/r 954158). The quarry appears to be active, in spite of the "dis" on the OS Explorer map.

The walk: south of Duncton, the escarpment turns sharply from its normal east-west course to run north-south for three kilometres, creating a sharp corner. The walk explores this corner and the downs south of it.

Shorter walk: start at Littleton Farm on the A285, where roadside parking is possible (m/r 950144). On the return, follow the outward route from the NT property on Bignor Hill,

---

1. Follow the track W towards the quarry. Just before the gate, two rights of way go off to the left (100m). Take the path on the left through woodland, parallel to the A285. Continue S across a field (300m), contouring to the right, and aim just right of the bottom of a wood (300m). Continue through the wood along a grassy path, then bear left (130m) between fields. Pass the track to Dogkennel Cottages (70m) and continue to a T-junction of tracks above **Littleton Farm** (550m). Turn left and go down to the farm and the A285 (200m).

2. Turn right, cross the road and follow a track on the left (30m) (the SDW) SE, uphill and round a zigzag into woodland (550m). Pass a track on the left and continue uphill with fields on the right and then on both sides. Pass the summit of **Sutton Down** on the right (1,100m). Continue through woodland to a junction of tracks and a NT sign *Slindon Estate* (400m). Continue along the edge of a field with radio towers on the left. Continue across an old earthwork (600m) to the junction of the SDW with *Stane Street* (120m).

3. Turn sharply back to the right along the Roman road, and follow it SW in virtually a straight line for nearly two-and-a-half kilometres. Just into **North Wood** there is a large signpost (2,300m) and a junction of six tracks which is also visited in Walk 10. There are three

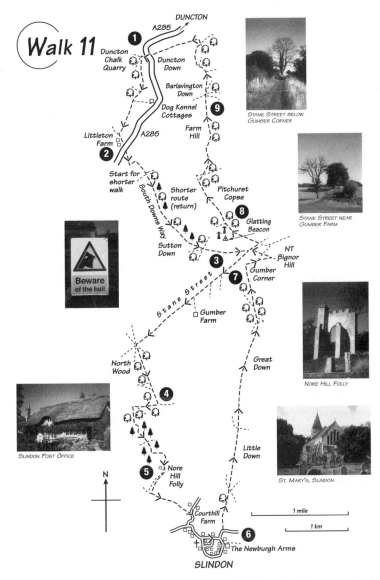

Walk 11

DUNCTON

A285

Duncton Chalk Quarry

Duncton Down

Barlavington Down

Dog Kennel Cottages

Littleton Farm

A285

Farm Hill

Start for shorter walk

South Downs Way

Shorter route (return)

Pitchurst Copse

Glatting Beacon

Sutton Down

Stane Street

NT Bignor Hill

Gumber Corner

Gumber Farm

Beware of the bull

North Wood

Great Down

Slindon Post Office

Little Down

Nore Hill Folly

N

Courthill Farm

SLINDON

The Newburgh Arms

1 mile

1 km

STANE STREET BELOW GUMBER CORNER

STANE STREET NEAR GUMBER FARM

NORE HILL FOLLY

ST. MARY'S, SLINDON

tracks on the left; take the central one and follow it SSE to a field on the left (650m). Continue to a junction of tracks (300m).

4. Turn right and follow a track W through woodland, downhill and then up, over a crossing path (320m). Continue uphill and turn left

along a path (80m) going uphill. At the top continue past a path on the right (300m) and another on the left (30m) and bear round to the right. Continue to a fork (80m), and turn left along a path which runs SE in a straight line for some distance and then swings left (400m) and right and into open country (120m). Join a track and follow it round to the right to *Nore Hill Folly* and a triangulation pillar (270m).

5. From this point, the track is not the RoW. Take a path on the left and follow it to a stile (30m). Turn right and go downhill along the edges of fields beside the track, and turn left at the bottom (450m). Continue to a lane by **Courthill Farm** (700m) and turn right. Turn left at a junction (250m) and continue into *Slindon*. Keep left at a small roundabout (330m) (turn right to visit the church) and continue to the inn (330m).

6. **Return:** from the inn, turn right along Top Road and right again along Mill Lane (80m). Where the lane turns right (150m) keep straight on along a track. Keep right at a fork (550m) and continue through a gate with a sign *Bridle Road To Bignor* (60m). The next section of the walk is excellent. Keep on in almost a straight line, heading N, between fences, over **Little Down** and **Great Down**. Continue into woodland (2,600m) and then beside a field on the right (450m). At its end turn right at a T-junction (450m).

7. Continue with woodland on the left. By a wooden seat (200m) turn left along a path into the wood. Turn left again along a crossing path (130m) and continue over another crossing path to the point where Stane Street was joined on the outward route (200m). Walk through a gap in the agger and immediately turn sharply back to the right beside it. Turn left at a T-junction (150m), where Stane Street continues down the escarpment, and follow a track NW past the radio towers on the left (550m).

8. Continue downhill past a track on the left (130m). Go between fields and along the edge of **Pitchurst Copse**. Continue with a field on the right and at its corner take a path on the right (800m) into woodland. Turn right along a track (40m) and at a junction of three paths take the one on the left. Follow it downhill between fields and up to a gate, and bear right along a track (450m). Follow it round to the left as it climbs the side of **Farm Hill**. At the top of a rise (450m) continue N through a gate and downhill across a field.

9. At the bottom, cross a path (300m) and bear right with woodland on

Great Down

the right and a field on the left, past paths going off to the right. Go steeply uphill and continue through woodland, following the path round the slopes of **Barlavington Down**, above Barlavington Hanger. Go down into woodland and at a junction of paths turn left (950m). At another junction turn left again (120m). Continue WSW through the wood (400m), cross a field to the A285 (400m), and turn right back to the start (50m).

En route

Stane Street: see Walk 10.

Nore Hill Folly: now a ruin, was built in the XVIII century as a summer house for Slindon Park.

Slindon: SLINDON COLLEGE was once SLINDON HOUSE. The CHURCH OF ST MARY contains a wooden effigy, unique in Sussex, of a warrior in the armour of the Wars of the Roses. The modern Roman Catholic CHURCH OF ST RICHARD is locked. There are many picturesque cottages. The inn is THE NEWBURGH ARMS.

Glatting Beacon: the hill with the radio towers (grid square SU 9613) is not named on any maps or in any guide books that I have seen. After enquiries from the OS and among locals had drawn a blank, James Fisher of the Sussex Downs Conservation Board supplied the name, discovered by Martin Bond on old maps. The OS plan to show it on future Explorer maps.

Walk 12

Houghton, Arundel (L), Fairmile Bottom

ــ   ɔut 11.0 km, 7.0 miles; return 9.0 km, 5.5 miles

Ascent: t 160m; return 310m

Times: out 2:50; return 2:35

Maps: Explorer 121, Landranger 197

Parking: car park on Bignor Hill (m/r 974129). The lane leading to it from Jay's Farm at Bignor is not signposted, and is rough enough to be mistaken for a farm track.

The walk: explores the area between Bignor and Arundel, and visits the town and the Park. It gives a mixture of woodland and downland typical of this area.

Shorter walk: park where the SDW crosses the A29 below Bury Hill (m/r 004118) and follow the outward route. On the return, follow the route shown on the map in Houghton Forest.

Caution: heavy rain may cause the Arun to flood and make the riverside route below Houghton impassable.

---

1. From the car park go ENE along an unfenced track (this is the SDW, which is followed to Houghton) and over ***Bignor Hill*** (800m). Follow the track round to the right, and turn left downhill (650m). Bear right at the bottom, zigzag left and right and continue past a group of barns (350m). Bear right uphill, continue SE over **Westburton Hill** and **Bury Hill**, and descend to the A29 (2,000m).

2. Turn right and shortly left (80m) and follow a track downhill (E) and round curves to a lane (1,500m). Turn right into ***Houghton*** (350m). At the B2139, turn right and left (10m) down South Lane to the River Arun (250m). Bear right and follow a path WSW along the west bank. At a bend the wall round **Arundel Park** appears. There are some impressive cliffs at this point, better seen from the park. Follow the riverside path until the wall bends to the right away from the river (1,300m), then go through a kissing gate into the park (45m).

3. Turn left and follow a path SW uphill, at first with the wall on the left. Continue with mature woodland on the right and a plantation (which may not be shown on the map) on the left. Turn right along a crossing track (250m) and at a junction (150m) follow it round to the left. At the top, pause to enjoy the view, cross a stile and continue S

to the right-hand side of **Dry Lodge Plantation** (450m), which strad-
dles the ridge.

4. Join a track and follow it with the plantation on the left. Where the
   track swings left (130m), bear right to a clump of box trees – there is

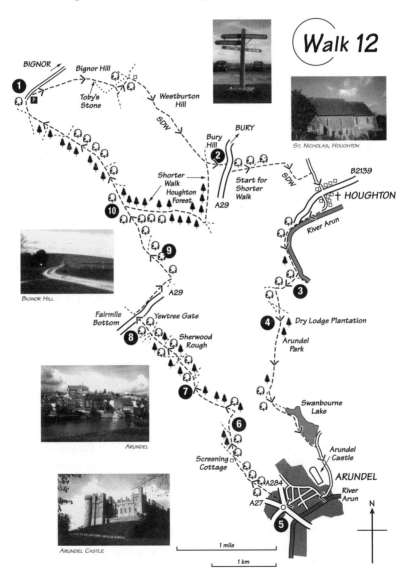

no path. Continue S below the ridge to a pair of box trees, go downhill to a junction of tracks (1,000m), and bear left along the valley bottom. At a fork (180m) keep right, and continue with **Swanbourne Lake** on the left. Continue to a road (950m), turn right and walk into *Arundel* (850m).

5. **Return:** walk to the roundabout at the end of Maltravers Street, at the west end of the town (700m). Cross the A284 and turn right up the A27 (80m). Immediately take a lane signposted *Chalk Springs Trout Farm and Fly Fishery* between two bungalows. By a similar sign (35m), take a track on the left going NW uphill into woodland. At the top (650m), follow the track round to the right. At a junction of tracks (270m) continue along the ridge.

6. Just past **Screening Cottage** (100m) take a path going downhill to the right. At the bottom (300m), continue over a crossing track and go uphill between fields to woodland. Turn left at a junction of tracks (370m) and continue NW with woodland on the right and a field on the left. Follow the track down into a dip and keep left at a fork (600m) (the track on the right, and the next one, may not appear on the map).

7. For the next one-and-a half kilometres, numerous tracks and paths can be confusing – remember that the route goes consistently NW. Walk uphill into **Sherwood Rough**, pass a track on the right (150m), and take a path on the left (40m). Follow the path past some yews, where it becomes indistinct, then go downhill. Cross a path at the bottom (500m) and go uphill to a junction of tracks (350m). Bear left along a track and then take a path on the right (50m). Continue uphill to a sign *Yewtree Gate* (200m). This is **Fairmile Bottom**, a Local Nature Reserve. Continue over crossing paths and go downhill, where steps assist the steeper part of the descent, to a car park and the **A29** (300m).

8. Cross, turn left, and take a path on the right (20m). Go downhill and just before a stile turn right (80m), and follow a path parallel to the road. The map may show woodland on the right, but the area is now a field. Continue into woodland, where a path joins from the right. Continue round to the left (750m), go downhill, and then up to a lane (230m).

9. Cross and continue along a path. There is now a long uphill trudge NW. Directions are not really necessary, but passing landmarks may help to relieve any tedium. Follow the track along the edge of

the wood. Keep left at a fork (250m) and continue to join a grassy track (850m), which is a cycle-way. The shorter route turns right along this.

10. Continue over a crossing track and past a track on the right, where the cycle-way leaves (600m). Follow the track gently round to the left, past a bridleway on the right and a track on the left. At the corner of a field on the right (750m) continue into the NT **Bignor Hill** property. Continue to a junction of tracks at the corner of a wood (650m), turn right and follow a track back to the car park (250m).

En route

Bignor Hill: just east of the summit, TOBY'S STONE (aka TOBY'S GRAVE) was a mounting post commemorating a local huntsman. In 1999 it was in pieces.

Houghton: has flint, thatched and timber-framed buildings. To the east is the CHURCH OF ST NICHOLAS; to the west THE GEORGE AND DRAGON, where Charles II found time to pause for a beer during his flight after the Battle of Worcester in 1651. The SDW was diverted here to avoid the B2139. Since the detour also avoids both the inns, it is unlikely to gain universal acceptance.

Arundel: a historic town and popular tourist centre, crowded most weekends. A visit needs more time than can be allowed during the walk. The HIGH STREET is reputed to be the steepest in

Signpost on Stane Street

England. As well as the town itself, the main attractions are: THE CASTLE: open Apr-Oct, Sun-Fri. tel: 01903 882173. THE CATHEDRAL (Roman Catholic, built in the XIX century in Gothic style); THE CHURCH OF ST NICHOLAS (part Church of England, part Roman Catholic chapel entered from the castle); THE MUSEUM & HERITAGE CENTRE, open Apr-Sep, Mon-Sat a.m./p.m, Sun p.m. only, tel: 01903 882344; THE WILDFOWL AND WETLANDS TRUST, open daily, tel: 01903 883355. There are numerous places of refreshment.

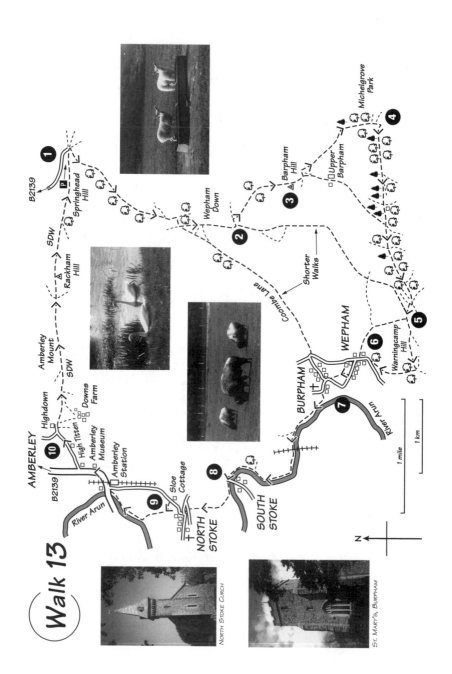

Walk 13

B2139

1

Springhead Hill

P

SDW

Rackham Hill

Amberley Mount

SDW

Highdown

Downs Farm

High Titten

Amberley Museum

AMBERLEY

B2139

River Arun

Amberley Station

10

Sloe Cottage

9

NORTH STOKE

8

SOUTH STOKE

River Arun

BURPHAM

WEPHAM

7

6

Warningcamp Hill

5

Wepham Down

2

Coombe Lane

Shorter Walks

Barpham Hill

3

Upper Barpham

4

Michelgrove Park

1 mile

1 km

N

North Stoke Church

St. Mary's, Burpham

Walk 13

Wepham Down, Burpham (L), River Arun, Rackham Hill

Distances: out 10.0 km, 6.5 miles; return 9.0 km, 5.5 miles

Ascent: out 70m; return 205m

Times: out 2:25; return 2:25

Maps: Explorer 121, Landranger 197

Parking: Kithurst Hill Car Park on main ridge SW of Storrington (m/r 070124). The lane to it from the B2139, half a kilometre east of Springhead Farm, is not signposted.

The walk: this walk explores both the main and secondary escarpments, and a secluded stretch of the River Arun. Time should be allowed for visits to the tiny hamlets of South and North Stoke.

Shorter walks: from Wepham Down, there are several shorter routes to Burpham – see map.

Caution: in wet conditions, floods may make paths beside the River Arun impassable.

---

1. The SDW runs past the car park, and two other RoWs go off to the south. Take a path on the right and go SW, at first between fields and then with woodland on the right (200m). Continue between fields (1,100m) and just before a wood (400m) turn right across a field. Turn left along the edge of the next field (130m) and in the next join a track. Continue S to **Wepham Down**, where there is a junction of tracks (750m).

2. A track joins from the right. Continue along a concrete track to the next junction (35m) and turn left. Follow a track to a gate on the right (120m), and follow a faint track SE up *Barpham Hill*. Continue through a patch of woodland (500m) and double gates, and bear right to the summit (500m).

3. Follow a made track to double gates (190m) and keep straight on over a T-junction (60m) to a path (10m). Turn left, and follow the path sharply round to the right to a metal gate (50m). Continue along a path running SE, above a steep escarpment on the left. At a gate (750m) follow the path round to the right and along the edge of a field. Continue through woodland (170m) and along a track which joins from the left, to a T-junction at **Michelgrove Park** (300m).

4. Turn right. There is now a long trudge W with little need for navigation. By buildings (1,100m), the track becomes metalled. Continue
to a point where tracks join from left and right (1,300) and there are
small fenced enclosures on either side. Just past these (35m) take a
path on the right going downhill. Continue over a crossing track and
join a track at the bottom (180m). Follow it round to the right to a
junction with another track (40m), and turn left.

5. Continue to a junction (100m), take a gate on the right and follow a
track along a bottom. Just past a row of tall ash trees, follow the track
round to the right (500m) and uphill to a metal gate. Where the track
swings left into a field (60m) continue uphill (N) along a path,
steeply at first, over **Warningcamp Hill**. At the top (250m) continue
across a field, bearing a little to the right. As Wepham comes into
sight, continue downhill into woodland (180m), bear right along a
path, follow it down to a lane (230m), and turn right.

6. Follow the lane into **Wepham**. Take a lane on the left (220m) and, at
the bottom of a hill, take a stile on the right (250m) above steps. Follow a path along the edge of a field, keep left along the edge of the
next, and in the third descend to cross a farm bridge to a lane (280m)
at *Burpham*. Turn right, then left at a T-junction, to the inn (200m).

7. Return: from the inn, face the church, turn left and walk W past St
Mary's Cottage. Go down a short dead-end lane and continue along
a path. At a fork keep right and follow a path down to the **River Arun**
(150m). In the field on the right, buffalo were grazing during both
my visits. Continue NW along the river bank to a fork (500m) by a
ruined building and keep left beside the river. Cross a railway
(250m) and continue along the embankment to a bridge at *South
Stoke* (1,250m), from where a visit may be made to the hamlet.

8. A little past the bridge the path leaves the Arun (150m). By a sign *5½
Knots* take a stile on the right and follow an embanked path to a footbridge (400m). At *North Stoke* continue across a track and follow a
path behind buildings (250m) to a lane (55m). Turn left and almost
immediately right (10m) along another lane. To visit the hamlet,
continue W. Follow the lane round to the right and to the left.

9. Just past **Sloe Cottage** take a path on the left (260m), follow it to the
Arun (500m) and turn right along the bank. Near *Houghton Bridge*,
bear left over a farm bridge to the B2139 (600m), and turn right. Continue under a railway bridge past *The Amberley Museum*. Take a

lane on the right, *High Titten* (500m), and begin a long climb up the ridge. This is the SDW, which is followed back to the start. Below **Highdown** (a house), a lane joins from the left (600m).

10. Follow the lane round a bend to the right and take a path on the left (100m). Immediately keep right and go steeply uphill to (E). Briefly follow a wide track by Downs Farm (400m) and continue up the hill. By a gate at the top (300m) a superb view to the west gives an excuse for a breather. There remains a relatively minor climb over **Amberley Mount** and **Rackham Hill** (triangulation pillar 1,200m). Parham House is seen below. Continue through a strip of woodland (750m) and over **Springhead Hill** to the car park (950m).

Houghton Bridge

En route

Barpham Hill: one of the attractive small hills produced by the secondary escarpment. The summit gives extensive views – Arundel Castle is seen to the SW and on the horizon, SSW, the white cliffs of the Isle of Purbeck. There is a triangulation pillar.

Burpham: means "the place by the fort". When the sea extended further inland the site was a stronghold against Viking raiders, and traces of the fort can be seen to the south of the village. The inn is THE GEORGE AND DRAGON (tel: 01903 883131). Opposite is the CHURCH OF ST MARY, which is mentioned in Domesday Book.

South Stoke: the tiny hamlet has ST LEONARD'S CHURCH, which is XI century. The walk just north of here follows the original course of the ARUN for a short distance. In 1839, it was shortened by a cut round South Stoke, when it formed part of the ARUN NAVIGATION. Later, when the railway was built, a similar cut was made round OFFHAM, to avoid the need for swing bridges.

North Stoke: the CHURCH (dedication unknown) is used only occasionally for services, and is maintained by the Churches Conservation Trust.

Houghton Bridge: has THE BRIDGE INN, THE BOATHOUSE RIVERSIDE BRASSERIE and HOUGHTON BRIDGE TEA GARDENS.

Amberley Museum: an industrial museum housed in an old chalk pit, which prides itself on exhibits that work. Open mid-March to October, Wed-Sun, daily in school holidays (tel: 01798 831370). A visit needs more time than can be allowed during this walk.

High Titten: near the top of the hill there is a grassy space on the right with a shelter and a seat, from which there are views over the museum. Further up, there are views of Amberley Castle.

Walk 14

Michelgrove, Selden (L), Patching

Distances: out 10.5 km, 6.5 miles; return 9.0 km, 5.5 miles

Ascent: out 210m; return 220m

Times: out 2:45; return 2:25

Maps: Explorer 121, Landranger 197, 198

Parking: on the east side of the A24, there is parking on the old road, and a car park a little way up the SDW (m/r 120120). There is limited parking on the west side of the A24.

The walk: visits some varied and pleasant countryside, but lacks any real highlights.

Shorter walk: just N of Michelgrove House, go E through Myrtle Grove Farm to join the return route. This by-passes the lunch stop.

---

1. The first part of the walk follows the SDW to Chantry Post. From the west side of the A24 walk up Glaseby Lane. Follow it round to the left (150m) and continue W along a track over **Highden Hill**. On **Barnsfarm Hill**, where the more obvious track swings left at the corner of a field (1,700m), keep straight on along the edge of a field. Continue past a barn (750m) and WNW over **Sullington Hill** to **Chantry Post** and a car park (850m), where two RoWs leave to the south. Take the one on the right, a grassy track along the edge of a field, and follow it SE. At the foot of Harrow Hill bear right towards **Lee Farm**.

2. Go through double metal gates by a barn and turn left (1,900m). Take the next gate immediately on the left by a sign *Angmering Park No Public Bridleway* – the metalled track is not a RoW. Turn right and follow a faint path S through a field, as the metalled track swings away to the right. There are more fences, and consequently gates, in the next section than may be shown on the Explorer map. Continue along a track which ascends the flank of **Harrow Hill** and then swings round to the left to contour the hillside. Cross two fields to join the metalled track at a bend (1,300m), and continue S along it to a lane (750m) at **Michelgrove House**.

3. Follow the lane round to the left and take a track on the right (300m) across a field. Go into a wood (90m), bear left and go S uphill past a track on the left. Keep left at a fork (200m) and ascend more gently.

Go round to the right and at the top continue over a crossing track (300m). At a fork (70m) keep left and continue gently downhill (SSW) along a grassy track. At a T-junction turn right (600m), continue over crossing tracks, and go downhill to a junction of tracks (500m). Turn left and walk S to a lane at **Selden Farm** (550m), whose buildings are a good example of the combined use of brick and flint. Continue to a T-junction with the old A27 (650m), and *The Fox.*

4. **Return:** walk back down the lane. At the bottom of a dip, turn right just past a pond (400m). Follow the edge of a field E, with a fence on the right. At the corner cross a stile and continue along the edge of the next field with the fence now on the left. A little before the end of the field turn right to a stile (330m) and then left, to continue with woodland on the left. Cross a stile and continue into the wood (350m) (the kink in the RoW which may be shown on the map does not appear to exist on the ground). Cross a field to a lane (380m), and turn left into *Patching*. Follow the lane N through the village, where the church can be visited by a detour to the left.

5. Follow the lane to its end (600m). Ignoring two tracks, continue along a path with a fence on the right. At the corner of the fence round a reservoir (200m), cross a stile and continue downhill. Continue N along the edge of a field, cross a track by a gate (300m), and fork right (30m) to a stile (50m). Follow a path between scrub and over a patch of grass to a lane (100m).

6. Turn left by **Patching Livery Stables** (possibly shown as a poultry farm on the Explorer map) and follow the lane to a stile on the right (80m). Follow a path between fields and then over a large pathless field (fences which may be shown on the Explorer map have gone). First aim just right of the high point, and then (NNE) for the right-hand end of an old hedge, where there is a finger post. On reaching this (600m) turn right and follow power lines to a lane (250m).

7. Turn left and follow the lane towards **Long Furlong** (Longfurlong?) **Farm**. Pass the farm's sign (150m), turn right (25m), and go downhill (E) along the edge of a field to a group of beeches (280m). Continue uphill across a field and then (950m) between fences. Near **Tolmare Farm** turn left along a track (450m), take a track on the left (20m) and follow it to a junction of tracks near the A280 (200m). Turn right and then left along a path running WNW between fences.

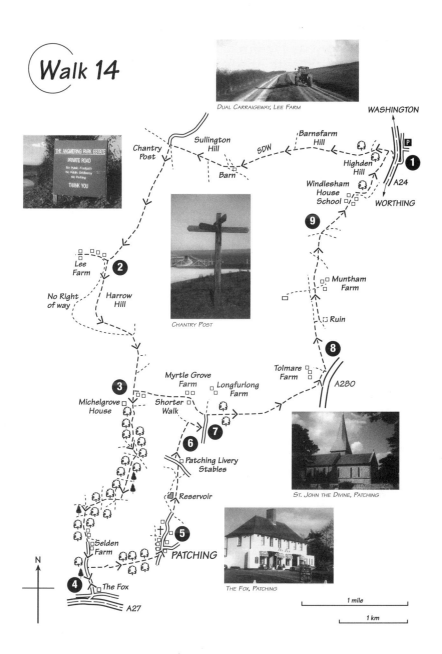

DUAL CARRAIGEWAY, LEE FARM

WASHINGTON

Sullington
Hill

Barnsfarm
Hill

Chantry
Post

SDW

Highden
Hill

Barn

Windlesham
House
School

A24

WORTHING

THE ANGMERING PARK ESTATE
PRIVATE ROAD
No Public Footpath
No Public Bridleway
No Parking
THANK YOU

Lee
Farm

No Right
of way

Harrow
Hill

Muntham
Farm

CHANTRY POST

Ruin

Myrtle Grove
Farm

Longfurlong
Farm

Tolmare
Farm

A280

Michelgrove
House

Shorter
Walk

Patching Livery
Stables

ST. JOHN THE DIVINE, PATCHING

Reservoir

Selden
Farm

PATCHING

N

The Fox

A27

THE FOX, PATCHING

1 mile

1 km

8. Follow the path to open ground (300m), and continue along a grassy track, where there are waymark posts. At the corner of a field go through a gate (450m), turn right and follow the edge of a field round to the left, past an ivy-covered ruin (50m). Continue N along the edge of the field with woodland on the right. Cross the concrete track to **Muntham Farm** (400m) and continue along the edge of the field. At its corner (450m) turn right through a gap, and then left to continue along the edge of a field. Follow the edge round to the right, and turn right along a track (320m).

9. Walk to a concrete track (20m) and turn left along it. Continue NE along the track through **Windlesham House School**, whose buildings are a mixture of the old and the new, until level with the last building. Take a track on the left (700m) and where it swings left into a field continue along a path to a metalled lane, the SDW (750m). Turn right back to the start (250m).

En route

The Fox: (tel: 01732 884808) offers good home-cooked food.

Patching: a small village with some attractive houses. The CHURCH OF ST JOHN THE DIVINE was reduced in size as the population shrank.

Thatched cottage at Patching

25/6/13 Short Route
Got Lost 4 hrs

Walk 15

Sompting Abbotts, Cissbury Ring, Findon (L), Steep Down

Distances: out 11.0 km, 6.5 miles; return 9.0 km, 5.5 miles

Ascent: out 290m; return 195m

Times: out 2:55; return 2:20

Maps: Explorer 121, 122, Landranger 198

Parking: a car park below Lancing Ring (m/r 182061) is not signposted. From the A27/A2025 roundabout, turn NW along a minor road signposted *N Lancing*. Take the first right, Mill Road, drive uphill and continue along a narrow lane to the car park.

The walk: the highlights are the unique church at Sompting Abbotts and the hill fort of Cissbury Ring – a circuit of the ramparts is recommended. Steep Down is an excellent viewpoint.

Shorter walk: from Findon, follow the outward route to the car park just N of Cissbury Ring. Continue E along a track to join the return route at Stump Bottom.

Caution: the annual sheep fair at Findon is held on the second Saturday in September.

---

1. From the car park follow a track or a path NW over **Lancing Ring,** a Local Nature Reserve. Go over the brow of the hill into open country, keeping close to a fence on the right. By a sign *Lancing Ring Local Nature Reserve* turn left (500m) and walk to a hedge (55m). Turn right and follow a path, which at first runs parallel to the previous one and then swings away. In the next field (600m), continue round to the left (W) following a sunken path in an old dyke. Go downhill (SW) along a track and bear left where another track joins at the bottom (850m). Turn right (300m) and follow a track NW to **Titch Hill Farm** (350m).

2. Turn left along a lane and follow it into *Sompting Abbotts* and the church (1,350m). A little past the church, turn right (100m) along a path, and then right again (180m) along another path, which goes uphill (N) between hedges. At the top turn left (500m) and at the next corner right (180m). Follow a path along the edge of a field and then past a patch of woodland near **Lambleys Barn.**

3. Turn right along a track (300m) and by **Coombe Barn** (200m), where the track swings right, continue NE along a thin path which swings

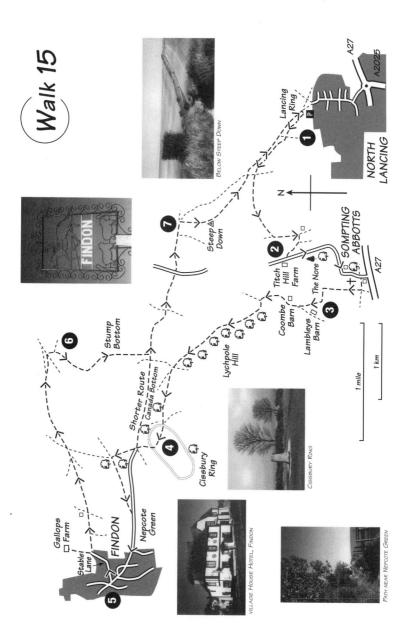

Walk 15

BELOW STEEP DOWN

FINDON

A27
A2025

Lancing
Ring

P

1

NORTH
LANCING

N

7

Steep
Down

2

SOMPTING
ABBOTTS

Titch
Hill
Farm

The Nore

A27

Coombe
Barn

Lambleys
Barn

3

Lychpole
Hill

Stump
Bottom

6

Shorter Route

Canada Bottom

1 km

1 mile

4

Cissbury
Ring

CISSBURY RING

Gallops
Farm

Stable
Lane

FINDON

Nepcote
Green

5

VILLAGE HOUSE HOTEL, FINDON

PATH NEAR NEPCOTE GREEN

to the left. Follow this down to the corner of a field (450m), go through the left-hand of two gates and turn left uphill to another gate (40m). Turn right along a faint path which runs along a field just below scrub and woodland on the flank of **Lychpole Hill**. Continue NW along the bottom of fields to a small wooden gate in a wire fence (1,350m). Continue to another gate (60m) and a NT sign *Cissbury Ring*. Take the left-hand of two paths and go uphill through trees and scrub. Where a path crosses, take a gate on the left just past a cattle-trough, and continue uphill to the ramparts of *Cissbury Ring* (650m), and then to the summit (200m).

4. From the triangulation pillar walk NW, and locate steps at the rampart (150m) which lead down towards a prominent white track and a car park. Go through the car park (200m) and along the track. Just past the corner of a field take a path on the left (350m) and follow it WSW to a road on the outskirts of *Findon* (850m). Continue past *Nepcote Green* and a road junction to a cross-roads in the centre of the village (1,000m).

5. **Return:** walk back along the road for a short distance, and take **Stable Lane** on the left (70m). Follow it uphill and round to the left to its end (450m) at a private road to Gallops Farm. Turn right along a track and follow it uphill (ENE), with good views of Cissbury Ring. Continue over a junction of tracks (1,400m) and along a narrower track. Go downhill and keep right where the track forks (1,100m).

6. At the bottom (220m), turn right and follow a grassy track S into **Stump Bottom**. Where it swings left (100m) continue along a path between overgrown hedges. Keep the hedge and later a fence on the left, continue to a crossing track (1,400m) and turn left (E). Keep left at a fork and continue over a crossing track (600m) to a road (500m). Cross and continue along a track, past another track on the right (480m), to a junction.

7. Bear right to a pylon (170m) and bear right again along a path leading S over **Steep Down**. The ascent can be avoided by following a track on the left round the side of the hill. Continue past the triangulation pillar on the summit (400m) and follow the path downhill. At the bottom (700m) turn left and then right (70m). Follow a path up to **Lancing Ring**, rejoin the outward route and follow it back to the car park (1,150m) – don't walk past it by mistake.

En route

Sompting Abbotts: the CHURCH OF ST MARY (open) has a Saxon Rhenish Helm tower, the only one in the country. Much of the church was built by the Knights Templar.

Cissbury Ring: a massive hill fort, covering 65 acres. It is named after the Saxon chief CISSA, but is much older. There are flint mines on the site whose products have been found as far away as the eastern Mediterranean. The summit has a triangulation pillar.

Nepcote Green: the site of an annual sheep fair, held here for centuries. The shuttered building at its edge was built to store hurdles.

Findon: a large village with an old centre and a good deal of continuing modern development. It has much to offer the visitor in search of refreshment. As well as THE GUN INN and THE VILLAGE HOUSE HOTEL (where horse racing memorabilia testify to famous stables nearby), there are bars, restaurants and shops. The CHURCH OF ST JOHN BAPTIST (locked) is a little way from the village on the other side of the A24.

St Mary's church, Sompting

Walk 16

Coombes, Wiston, Washington (L), Chanctonbury Ring

Distances: out 12.0 km, 7.5 miles; return 10.5 km, 6.5 miles

Ascent: out 275m; return 195m

Times: out 3:10; return 2:40

Maps: Explorer 121, 122, Landranger 198

Parking: on verges of road south of Church Farm, Coombes (m/r 192082)

The walk: follows one of the best sections of the SDW, including the famous Chanctonbury Ring, and also explores the foot of the escarpment.

Shorter walk: start at the lane from Steyning to Sompting Abbotts. Parking is available at junctions with tracks (m/rs 165088, 162094 and 165099), but there is no parking where the SDW joins the lane (m/r 162096).

---

1. Walk up the track through **Church Farm**. Where it turns right (100m), go through a gate on the left and uphill through a field past *Coombes Church* (100m). Continue into a wood and bear left uphill along a path. At the top (150m), turn sharply back to the right. Just past double metal gates take a small wooden gate on the right (60m) and follow a faint path W along the top of a field. Follow a fence round to the left past **Coombehead Wood** (950m). Looking back to the south east there is a good view of Lancing College Chapel. Continue WSW to a small wood on the left (1,150m), which may not be shown on the map.

2. Just past the wood, turn right (270m) and follow a track NNW to a lane (950m). Continue for a short distance to gates, where the SDW joins (100m), and follow a path beside the road. Continue above **Steyning Bowl**, cross the road where it bends right (750m), and continue along a track to the **Langmead Memorial**, a simple commemoration of a local farmer.

3. Go over a crossing track (350m) and immediately take a grassy path on the right, leaving the SDW. Follow the path NNE over the brow of **Steyning Round Hill**, and down to a crossing path (350m). Turn left and follow the path above a hanger. At a fork (550m) keep right, descend to another fork and keep left before a kissing gate (500m). Continue to another path (300m), turn right and follow it downhill.

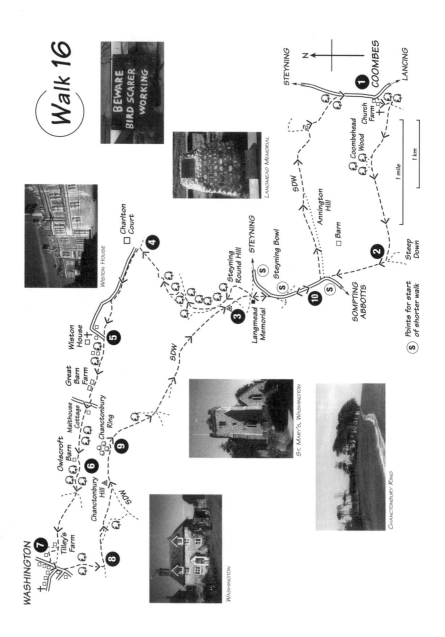

Walk 16

Near the bottom an apparent fork is only a shortcut. Continue NE between fields.

4. At the bottom, just before a lane, ascend steps on the left (800m) and follow a path along the edge of a field beside the lane. The rest of the outward route goes westwards to Washington. There are good views of the escarpment, with the remains of Chanctonbury Ring prominent at the far end. Continue along the path parallel to the lane, follow it round the corner of a field and turn right into a small wood (900m). Cross a footbridge and continue into a field (100m). Cross a stile, and continue along the edge of a field (not across it as the map may indicate) and then follow a track which runs beside the field. At a lane (500m), turn right to visit *Wiston* (200m).

5. To continue the walk, turn left and continue along the lane. Where its ends (200m), keep straight on by a metal gate. Continue through *Great Barn Farm* to a T-junction (800m) and turn right and almost immediately left (15m) by Malthouse Cottage. Follow a track along the foot of the escarpment and into a wood.

6. Pass **Owlscroft Barn** (850m) and follow the track round an uphill zigzag. At a fork (220m) keep right through a metal gate. At the corner of a field (270m), where the track swings left, take a small wooden gate on the right and follow a faint path across a field, bearing away from the escarpment. In the next field continue to the end of a hedge (500m) and continue with the hedge on the right. At farm buildings, (350m) pass a track on the right and continue to a stile on the right (50m). Follow a faint path across a field as houses appear. In the next field bear left across its corner, cross a concrete track and turn right along a path between fences. Cross a footbridge and bear right across a field to a road (350m) at *Washington* and turn right for the inn.

7. **Return:** from the inn turn right and follow the road, which is the old A24, to a lane on the right, The Street (200m see below). Continue to a road, Stocks Mead, and take a path on the left (90m). Cross two stiles and bear left across a field to the middle of a wood (160m). Follow a path uphill (S) through the wood, possibly to the accompaniment of noise from the quarry on the right.

8. The path meets a track, which is the SDW (500m). Turn left and immediately (10m) keep left at a fork. Just past a gas installation, pass a path on the left (300m) and continue uphill. Go through a wooden

gate on the left (100m) and follow a path steeply uphill through old chalk pits (for easier gradients follow the SDW round a dog-leg). Continue E through a gate and across almost pathless downland, with a few waymark posts, to a dewpond. Bear right to rejoin the track and the SDW (900m), and continue up Chanctonbury Hill to *Chanctonbury Ring* (550m).

9. The rest of the return route follows the SDW almost to the start. Keep left at a fork (950m) and follow the ridge SE to re-join the outward route at the **Langmead Memorial** (2,200m). Follow the track S to the road (350m), then follow the path beside the road to gates (750m), where the SDW goes off to the left.

10. Leave the outward route to follow the SDW, a thin path, E along the edge of a field and then across its corner over Annington Hill (1,300m). The route of the path is not quite that shown on the map – when the field was ploughed the path followed its edge. Continue along the edge of the next field, follow a track round a bend to the left by a house (1,000m), and turn right (30m) down to a gate (25m). Turn right and follow a path SE along the top of a field, passing below the house. Follow the edge of the field down into a small wood (750m), which is a disused tip and may not be shown on the map. Go into the wood, keep right and follow a path uphill to open ground. Bear left under power lines to a lane (100m). Turn right and follow the lane S back to the start (550m).

En route

Coombes: the CHURCH (dedication unknown) is famous for its wall paintings. It is locked, but the key can be had at the farmhouse.

Wiston: the Elizabethan WISTON HOUSE, still owned by the Goring family, is not open to the public, but can be seen from the outside. The adjacent CHURCH OF ST MICHAEL is open. See also CHANCTONBURY RING below.

Great Barn Farm: the barn is a fine example of the combined use of brick and flint, and has massive roof tiles.

Washington: the inn is THE FRANKLAND ARMS (tel: 01903 892220). THE STREET mentioned in the route description leads to the older part of the village. The bridge at its end provides a safe crossing of the A24, and is an alternative route for the SDW. ST. MARY'S CHURCH has two towers;

the old "Templars" tower was left standing when the "Bell" tower was added.

Chanctonbury Ring: one of the most famous points on the Downs. It has – or had – a grove of beeches, planted on the site of a hill fort (the Ring) in 1760 by young CHARLES GORING of WISTON HOUSE, who is reputed to have carried jugs of water up the hill to nurture the young trees. It was devastated by the hurricane of 1987, which left only the younger trees on the periphery standing. The fallen trees were cleared with minimal damage to the site, and it has been re-planted, but no one who knew it before can visit it now without a sense of loss.

Chanctonbury Ring

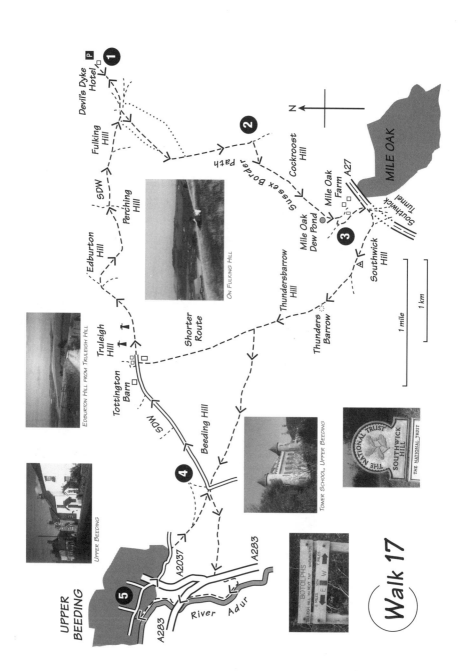

Devil's Dyke Hotel

Fulking Hill

SDW

Perching Hill

Edburton Hill

ON FULKING HILL

Truleigh Hill

EDBURTON HILL FROM TRULEIGH HILL

Shorter Route

Tottington Barn

SDW

Beeding Hill

UPPER BEEDING

UPPER BEEDING

A2037

A283

River Adur

A283

Cockroost Hill

Sussex Border Path

Mile Oak Farm

A27

MILE OAK

Southwick Tunnel

Mile Oak Dew Pond

Southwick Hill

Thundersbarrow Hill

Thunders Barrow

1 mile

1 km

TOWER SCHOOL, UPPER BEEDING

SOUTHWICK HILL THE NATIONAL TRUST

BOTOLPHS

Walk 17

Walk 17

Mile Oak, Thundersbarrow Hill, Upper Beeding (L), Truleigh Hill

Distances: out 12.0 km, 7.5 miles; return 7.5 km, 5.0 miles
Ascent: out 155m; return 300m
Times: out 2:55; return 2:15
Maps: Explorer 122, Landranger 198
Parking: car park at Devil's Dyke Hotel (m/r 258110)
The walk: long, open ridges give exhilarating walking. Extensive views are unfortunately marred by innumerable pylons, and Truleigh Hill is not the most attractive spot on the Downs.
Shorter walks: 1. Use the return route along the SDW as the outward route.
2. From Thundersbarrow Hill, continue N to join the return route on Truleigh Hill. This by-passes the lunch stop.

---

1. From the *Devil's Dyke Hotel*, follow the rim of the escarpment SW, past a ruined building on the left, to a gate with a NT sign *Fulking Escarpment* (800m) (the map may show a route SSW before this point, but it is barred by fences). Turn half left, follow a path SW, and in the next field (800m) bear left (SSE) along its edge.

2. Just after going under power lines (850m), which may not appear on the map, take a track on the right and follow it past *Mile Oak Dew Pond*. A little past the pond, where the track swings left to **Mile Oak Farm** (1,200m), continue along another track, downhill towards a pylon. At the bottom (300m), turn sharply back to the right, pass the pylon, and take a track on the left (60m).

3. Go uphill (SE) under power lines, first to the left and then to the right. Continue uphill to the crest of the ridge (700m), cross a stile, and turn right along a track. The walk now follows the ridge NW for over two kilometres. Continue past a NT sign *Southwick Hill* (150m) and continue past the triangulation pillar (500m) on **Southwick Hill**. At Thunders Barrow (700m) the track loses its fences. Continue over *Thundersbarrow Hill* to double metal gates and turn left (900m). Go down into a dip and up again (WNW) along the flank of **Beeding Hill** to cross a lane (2,000m).

4. From here it is possible to go straight down to the village by continuing WNW along a chalk track. For the full walk, take a gate on the left and follow a grassy path, the SDW, downhill towards the **River**

Adur. Cross the A283 (1,100m) and turn left. A little way along a lay-by, take a path on the right and follow it round to the right to a footbridge (350m). Do not cross; turn right along the east bank of the river. Continue under the A283 bridge (850m) and at the next bridge (650m) turn right into **Upper Beeding**.

5. **Return:** walk along the main street and keep right at a mini-round-about (400m). At another, by The Rising Sun (130m), turn left along the A2037. Just past a car breakers (450m), take a private road (a track) on the right and go ESE uphill to the lane crossed on the outward route (850m). From here, the SDW is followed almost to the start. Turn left, follow the lane NE to Tottington Barn Youth Hostel (1,550m) and continue past radio towers and buildings on **Truleigh Hill**. Follow the SDW to a junction below **Edburton Hill** (1,300m) and continue over **Perching Hill** to the gate used on the outward route (2,200). Follow the outward route back to the start (800m).

En route

The Devil's Dyke Hotel: has large bars, a family dining centre and public toilets. A very, very popular spot, particularly with hang-gliders. There is an excellent triple view indicator.

Mile Oak Dew Pond: a wooden plaque bears a quotation from Kipling. In spite of the wording, the pond is sometimes dry.

Southwick Hill: the walk passes above the tunnel cut for the new A27.

Thundersbarrow Hill: there are many ancient remains as well as the eponymous barrow.

Upper Beeding: has shops, an Indian take-away and three inns: THE BRIDGE, THE KING'S HEAD and THE RISING SUN (on the A2037). ST PETER'S CHURCH was originally built for the priory.

Truleigh Hill

Walk 18

Wolstonbury Hill, Newtimber Hill, Fulking (L), Varncombe Hill

Distances: out 10.5 km, 6.5 miles; return 9.5 km, 6.0 miles
Ascent: out 235m; return 340m
Times: out 2:45; return 2:45
Maps: Explorer 122, Landranger 198
Parking: on the old A23, now a dead-end, north of Pyecombe (m/r 288126).
The walk: on either side of Pyecombe two hills, Wolstonbury and Newtimber, protrude from the main ridge. The walk visits both, and goes on to explore the escarpment and the dip slope to the south.
Shorter walks: 1. On the outward route, follow the lane from Poynings to Fulking. 2. On the return, join the SDW above Fulking and follow it back to Pyecombe (see Walk 20 for route description).

---

1. From the old A23, take a road signposted *Haresdean* and *Newtimber*, which loops round to bridge the new A23. A made path on the left (which may still be shown as a road on the map) is signposted as a cycle-way *Pyecombe and Hassocks*, and is taken as the starting point. Follow the path past the church at *Pyecombe.* At a road junction, (250m) turn left along The Wyshe and continue N along a path. Continue to a track (720m) and a NT sign *Wolstonbury Hill.* Cross the track, which is not the RoW, and turn left through a gate. Follow a path W near the edge of a field and join the track. Follow the track until it begins to descend, then turn right (800m) to the summit of **Wolstonbury Hill** (280m).

2. From the summit turn left and go SW along a grassy path, aiming just left of a chalk pit. Cross a stile (130m), turn left and follow a thin path beside a fence. Join a more obvious path and turn sharply back right (130m). Just past a dyke running down the hillside (300m), keep left at a fork. Go downhill into woodland and by a NT sign (100m), turn sharply back left through a gate. Follow a path along the flank of the hill, join a track (700m), and continue SE to the northern part of *Pyecombe.*

3. Cross a footbridge over the A23 (400m), and continue uphill (SW) along the edge of a field. A house and stables were being built here in 1999. In the next field (350m) bear right along its edge. Continue along the edge of a wood (280m), go through a gate (270m), and follow a grassy path W to the summit of **Newtimber Hill** (400m).

4. Follow a faint path round to the left to **North Hill** (500m), then descend S towards Saddlescombe. Cross a track by a gate (450m), follow a sunken path to a junction of tracks (60m), and turn sharp right to a road (50m).

5. Cross and turn right along a path which first runs beside the road and then descends through a hanger. Join the drive of a house and continue to a road (650m). Turn left into **Poynings** (see Walk 20) and follow the road past the church. Keep left at a road junction by the church, then cross the road to a stone arch and a path above the road (250m).

6. Just ahead The Royal Oak offers an alternative lunch stop. From here it is possible to go directly to Fulking by the road, which the full walk avoids. Take a wooden kissing gate on the right (150m) and follow a path NW beside a fence. Continue through a metal kissing gate and bear right (250m) along a made path. Go through a wooden kissing gate and turn left (40m) along a path behind houses. At a concrete track, **Mill Lane**, turn left (100m) and follow it between houses into open country. There are good views of the escarpment on the next section of the walk.

7. At a junction of tracks by a sewage works, continue W beside a stream. Cross the stream by a farm bridge (450m) and bear left towards a stile. Bear right across a field, aiming for a pylon, and cross a smaller field to a lane (750m). Turn right, and just over a bridge take a path on the left (170m), to the left of a concrete track. Follow the path beside a stream and over a footbridge (160m), then turn left (40m) over another footbridge. Bear left to the corner of a field near stables, then bear right along its edge.

8. Cross a footbridge (100m) and continue S along the edge of a field, following power lines. Cross a track (300m) and continue along the edge of another field. At its end, by houses on the left, cross a stile (350m) and turn right through a kissing gate. Follow the edge of a field to a corner (90m) then bear left across another field. Bear left along the edge of the next field to a lane (250m), then turn right and follow the lane to the inn (80m) at **Fulking**.

9. **Return:** from the back of the inn's car park follow a path S to the foot of the escarpment (250m). Cross a stile and climb steps to a NT sign

Walk 18

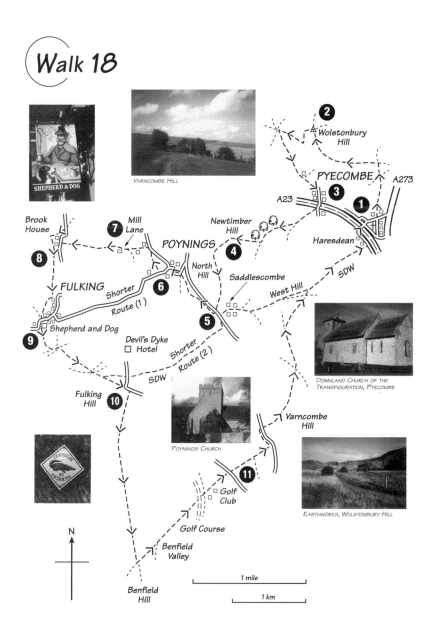

VARNCOMBE HILL

DOWNLAND CHURCH OF THE
TRANSFIGURATION, PYECOMBE

POYNINGS CHURCH

EARTHWORKS, WOLSTONBURY HILL

SHEPHERD & DOG

2 Wolstonbury Hill

PYECOMBE A273

A23 **3** **1**

Brook House   Mill Lane **7**   Newtimber Hill   Haresdean

POYNINGS **4**

8   North Hill   Saddlescombe

FULKING   Shorter   **6**   West Hill   SDW

Route (1)   **5**

Shepherd and Dog

9   Devil's Dyke □ Hotel   Shorter Route (2)

SDW

Fulking Hill **10**   Varncombe Hill

11

Golf Club

Golf Course

N

Benfield Valley

Benfield Hill

1 mile

1 km

Fulking Escarpment. Bear left, climb steeply across the escarpment and cross a sunken track (180m). Continue the ascending traverse to the ridge on **Fulking Hill**, where the path peters out. As the sea comes into view, continue SE to a fence (600m) and bear left beside it to a road (380m).

10. Almost immediately turn right (10m) along a track, which later becomes a path. There is now a long, uninterrupted walk S to a junction of tracks below **Benfield Hill** (2,150m). Turn left and go downhill into **Benfield Valley** (350m), and then NE up beside a golf course. Cross the course of the old Dyke Railway (800m), about which there is a signboard. Continue past the clubhouse along a metalled track and cross a road (500m).

11. Continue NE across a field, and then another to its right-hand corner. Turn left before a stile (650m) and walk beside the road to a stile on the right (170m). Follow the road for a short distance, then take a track on the right (50m) and follow it NE up onto **Varncombe Hill**. Continue over a junction (950m) with the Sussex Border Path, bear left, then follow the track round to the right below the summit, ignoring a path going straight on (550m). Continue uphill, then descend NE a little to a junction of tracks by a gate (500m). Follow a track, the SDW, down towards the A23. Turn left (1,100m), cross the road bridge (250m), and go round to the left and back to the start (150m).

En route

Pyecombe: is in two halves, nearly a kilometre apart, the result of villages fleeing an outbreak of plague in 1603. It is a pleasant village, but too near to busy roads. All the following are in the southern part. The DOWNLAND CHURCH OF THE TRANSFIGURATION has a centrally-hinged tapsell gate which incorporates a shepherd's crook, for the manufacture of which the village was once celebrated. THE PLOUGH INN is at the end of the lane running S from the church – this was once the main road to Brighton. Near the church, the OLD FORGE TEA ROOMS are open at weekends and bank holidays (and by appointment for walking groups, tel: 01273 842272). The famous shepherd's crooks were once made here.

Wolstonbury Hill: has the usual fort, and is pockmarked with the remains of flint mines, plus some XIX century diggings. The summit, which has a triangulation pillar, is one of the best. Because the hill pro-

Wolstonbury Hill

trudes from the main ridge, the views to the west are superb. Walk a little to the north to see DANNY below.

Newtimber Hill: trees and scrub obstruct much of the outlook. Its subsidiary summit, NORTH HILL gives a better view, which includes THE DEVIL'S DYKE.

Fulking: the famous SHEPHERD AND DOG inn is very popular at weekends, but does not take bookings. There is an equally famous SPRING and PUMP HOUSE nearby, and a fountain can be seen just after entering the village. There is no church; the cross on the map is a small chapel.

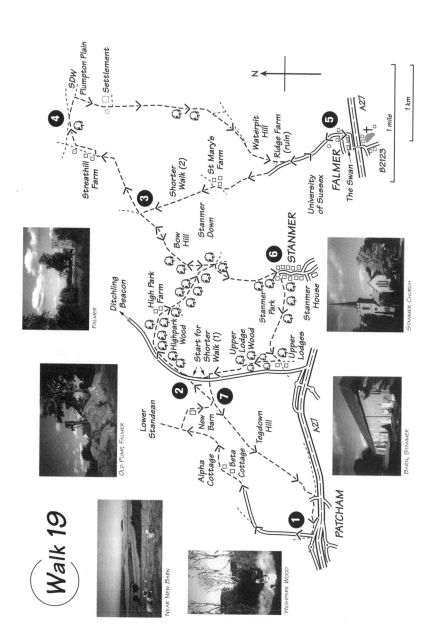

Walk 19

Walk 19

High Park, Plumpton Plain, Falmer (L), Stanmer

Distances: out 12.5 km, 7.5 miles; return 10.5 km, 6.5 miles

Ascent: out 270m; return 270m

Times: out 3:15; return 2:50

Maps: Explorer 122, Landranger 198

Parking: on minor road (Braypool Lane) above the A27 roundabouts (m/r 302094)

The walk: the northward expansion of Brighton has left a strip of open downland little more than two-and-a-half miles deep. Exploration of this area is worth while, but requires some dodging about. It is to be hoped that there will be no further development north of the A27.

Shorter walks: 1. Start at Ditchling Road. There is limited parking at the two points where the walk crosses (m/rs 322107 and 322111). 2. On the outward route, from Bow Hill, follow the return route to Stanmer.

---

1. From the top of a rise, follow a lane N and then round to the right. Chattri is seen ahead (see Walk 20). Go past **Beta and Alpha cottages** (1,400m) and, just after the buildings of Lower Standean come into sight ahead, take a track on the right (1,000m). Follow it uphill (ESE) to **New Barn**. Go round to the right past the barn (300m) and continue uphill through a gate and round to the left. Where power lines join by a gate (350m), leave the track and bear left (NE) across a pathless field, ascending only slightly. Cross a stile and the corner of another field to a road (500m).

2. Cross the road, turn left, and follow a path which runs parallel to it through woodland. Where the path forks (550m), keep right and follow it away from the road. Keep left where a path goes off right (200m) and continue past **High Park Farm** (200m), which in summer is barely visible through foliage. Go downhill (SE), and at a junction of tracks (950m), turn sharply left and continue downhill (N) through a hanger. At the bottom (400m), continue along the edge of a field. At its corner (200m) go through a small wooden gate and continue along a bottom below **Bow Hill**, with a fence on the left. Follow the path uphill, away from the fence, to a junction with another (600m).

3. Continue NE across the corner of a field (150m) and across the next, bearing a little to the right. Continue over the brow of a hill to the edge of the field (600m) and turn left towards **Streathill Farm**. By a redbrick bungalow (300m) move to the right and follow a path which is the RoW, not the metalled track to the farm. By a large house (250m), bear right along a path across the corner of a field, and follow it to two old gate posts (400m).

4. Turn right (E) and follow a track, the SDW, over **Plumpton Plain**, and take the first track on the right (230m). Continue past a field on the left (450m), where there are traces of a settlement, and continue S. Descend to a bottom (1,250m) and, at a fork, bear right (SW) along a path which ascends the flank of **Waterpit Hill**. At the top (600m), there is an aerial view of St. Mary's farm to the west. Join another path and continue along the edge of a field. Join a lane (700m) by some derelict buildings, named as **Ridge Farm** on the Explorer map. Turn left and walk into *Falmer*, keeping left at a junction (850m). Follow the road round to the right to the inn (220m).

5. **Return:** follow the lane back to the junction where it was joined (970m), keep left and continue down to **St. Mary's Farm**. Just past the buildings (1,000m) bear slightly left by double metal gates and follow a track uphill (NNW) along the edge of a field and over **Stanmer Down**. Go past gates on the brow of the hill (850m) to a gate on the left (150m) and turn left along the outward route. Go down to and along a bottom. Continue with a wood on the right, then go into the wood (800) and uphill to a junction (400m), where the outward route is left. Continue SSE along a track between fields. Go downhill and bear left at the bottom. Go between farm buildings to a lane (950m) and a pond. To visit *Stanmer* continue along the lane (300m).

6. Follow the lane back, round to the left by the pond (300m), and uphill (W). As a house (one of two **Upper Lodges**) comes into view (1,150m) a track goes off on the right. Follow it (not the path to its right) round to the right and uphill (N) though Upper Lodge Wood. Cross two stiles at the corner of a field (500m) and continue along the edge of a field parallel to a road. By power lines (450m) turn left to cross a road (50m) and follow the power lines beside a fence.

7. At a gate on the left (300m), which was visited on the outward route, turn half left and continue SW with a fence on the left (the RoW is the path, not the track in the next field). At the end of a field (400m)

Above Falmer

go through a small wooden gate and continue along a path with fences on each side. Cross a stile onto downland and keep straight on over **Tegdown Hill** along the faintest of paths. By a dewpond on the right (350m) bear slightly left to a stile beside metal gates (300m). Follow a track towards the A27, turn right (650m) along a minor road, and walk back to the start past a travellers' site (550m).

En route

Falmer: was cut in two by the new A27. THE SWAN INN is in the northern part. The southern half, which is very attractive, can be reached by a footbridge. There is a green with a pond, the old pump, several flint houses and the CHURCH OF ST. LAURENCE (locked). COURT FARM has a splendid barn.

Stanmer: a good example of an estate village. There are attractive cottages and a massive weather-boarded barn; also a CAFÉ, RESTAURANT and VILLAGE STORES (tel: 01273 604 041) and toilets. STANMER PARK, once the seat of the Earls of Chichester, and famous for its landscaping, is now partly occupied by the UNIVERSITY OF SUSSEX. STANMER HOUSE (not open to the public) stands opposite the CHURCH (locked), which is XIX century.

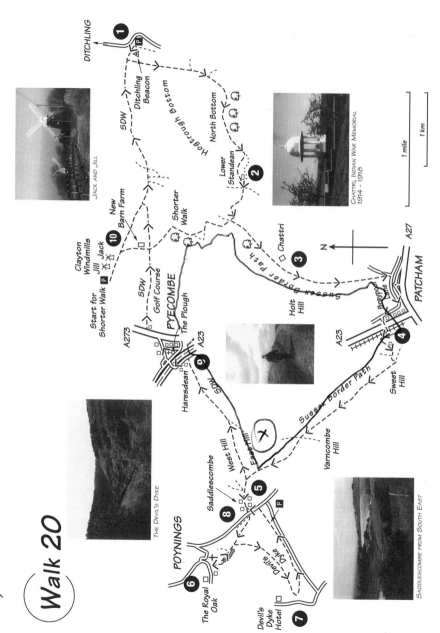

JACK AND JILL

CHATTRI, INDIAN WAR MEMORIAL 1914 - 1918

THE DEVIL'S DYKE

SADDLESCOMBE FROM SOUTH EAST

1 mile

1 km

N

Walk 20

SDW 2½ miles 8½ hours

9/3/14

DITCHLING

SDW

Ditchling Beacon

Hogtrough Bottom

North Bottom

Lower Standean

Chattri

Sussex Border Path

Holt Hill

PATCHAM

A27

A23

Braypool Lane

Sweet Hill

Varncombe Hill

Sussex Border Path

New Barn Farm

Shorter Walk

Clayton Windmills

Jill Jack

Start for Shorter Walk

SDW

Golf Course

PYECOMBE

The Plough

A273

A23

Haresdean

SDW

West Hill

East Hill

Saddlescombe

POYNINGS

The Royal Oak

Devil's Dyke

Devil's Dyke Hotel

Walk 20

Ditchling Beacon, Saddlescombe, Poynings (L), Devil's Dyke

Distances: out 11.5 km, 7.5 miles; return 10.5 km, 6.5 miles

Ascent: out 325m; return 265m

Times: out 3:10; return 2:50

Maps: Explorer 122, Landranger 198

Parking: Ditchling Beacon car park (NT), small charge, on minor road south of Ditchling (m/r 333130)

The walk: the A23 makes a great gash through the Downs – between the road bridge at Pyecombe and the footbridge north of Patcham there is only one crossing, at Pangdean, and this is of no use to walkers because there is no RoW on the eastern side. The walk explores this area, which has many places of interest. Navigation on the first section requires care as the sign-posted RoWs are not always as shown on the map.

Shorter walk: start at the Clayton Windmills, where there is a car park, and follow a track S to join the outward route west of Lower Standean.

---

1. From the car park at ***Ditchling Beacon***, walk WNW along the SDW. Descend a little, take a gate on the left (350m), and follow a path S between fields. Continue above Hogtrough Bottom, descend to a gate (850m), and bear right along a grassy path into **North Bottom**. The woodland on the left does not extend to the path as the map may indicate. Follow the path round to the left past a metal gate on the right (1,050m). For the next 1,300 metres signposted RoWs may not be as shown in the map. Take a wooden gate on the right (100m) beside double metal gates, and follow a track which first runs SW beside the fence and then swings uphill to the right. Follow the track round to the left and downhill to a junction above **Lower Standean** (750m).

2. Turn right and follow a track uphill towards a small barn. Just before the barn, move right by a gate (300m) and follow a path which runs beside the track. Continue into a field, turn left (130m) and follow its edge round to the right. On the crest of the ridge turn left along a track (150m) and continue a past a clump of sycamores. This is the Sussex Border Path, which is followed to Saddlescombe. The urban coastal sprawl appears ahead, and then, down on the left,

Hogtrough Bottom

Chattri. Continue SW into the next field (900m), where Chattri may be visited by walking down to the left.

3. Continue along the top of the field, and across the next to its far end and a minor road above the A27, **Braypool Lane** (1,500m). Turn right and follow the lane above a roundabout and round to the right. Just past Ben-Ma-Chree, turn left (700m) over a footbridge and cross the A23 and the railway (180m).

4. Follow the path round to the right (130m), then turn left and right (10m) to join a track, which goes round to the left and uphill. At a T-junction turn right (500m) and continue NW over **Varncombe Hill.** Where the track swings right and another joins on the left (1,600m), keep straight on NW across a field, and then along the lower edge of the next. At a zigzag in the fence (550m) continue along the lower edge of another field. At a group of three gates (400m), the path joins the SDW. Bear left downhill to **Saddlescombe.** Just before the buildings, a detour to the left may be made to visit the donkey wheel. Continue along a track, keeping the farm buildings on the left, and just past them turn left down to a gate (350m). Turn right along a track (50m) and continue to a road.

5. Cross to a metalled path and follow it downhill. As a house comes into view ahead (300m), take a grassy path on the left and follow it along the bottom of a field to a corner, where it drops to the right. Continue to a stile, descend steps to a crossing path (200m), and turn right (to omit the visit to Poynings, turn left up to the Devil's Dyke). Follow the path round to the left to a pond, which is often partly dry. At a fork (130m), keep left beside the pond. Turn left across the dam and then left along the edge of a field. Continue past a garage to the road at **Poynings** (400m) and turn left to the inn (100m).

6. **Return:** from the inn turn left and walk back through the garage, the field and beside the pond. Just past the pond, (630m) continue S uphill to a gate and a NT sign *Devil's Dyke*. Continue along the bottom of the Dyke (a permissive path), then climb strenuously up the end of the hollow, keeping left near the top. Follow a fence to a stile, from where a detour can be made to the Devil's Dyke Hotel. By gates (1,200m), turn left along the SDW, which is followed for most of the rest of the walk. Keep left at a fork and continue E with the Dyke on the left. Just before a car park bear left (1,000m) and continue down to a road (550m). Cross and follow a private road towards *Saddlescombe*, where the outward route is rejoined briefly.

7. Take a path on the left (80m) by a NT sign *Newtimber Hill*, join a track and continue past the farm. At the junction of three gates (350m), leave the outward route by continuing uphill (ENE), with a fence on the right. Continue over **West Hill** and down (NE) to the A23 (1,850m).

8. Turn left past the Brendon Horse & Rider Centre at **Haresdean** and then right (250m) to cross the A23 by the road bridge. Turn right along a path (200m) and cycle-way (still shown as a road on some maps) to **Pyecombe** (see Walk 18). Continue along a lane by the church to the A273 (400m), and turn left along a path. At its end (200m) cross the road and walk up the drive to **Pyecombe Golf Club**. At the car park (100m) bear left along a track and go uphill (E) through the golf course. At the corner of the course (1,050m) keep straight on (to visit the *Clayton Windmills*, turn left past New Barn Farm and left again at a T-junction). Follow the path round to the left, turn right at a junction (550m), and follow the SDW back to *Ditchling Beacon* (2,300m).

En route

Ditchling Beacon: is the third highest point on the South Downs, with its triangulation pillar at 814 feet (246 metres). There is a popular car park, complete with ice-cream van for much of the year.

Chattri must be the most unexpected building on the Downs. In the First World War, Indian Hindu and Sikh soldiers who were wounded on the Western Front were nursed in the Royal Pavilion, then a war hospital, in Brighton. Those who died were cremated here, and this is their memorial.

Saddlescombe: (pronounced *Sa'lscum*) a tiny hamlet, whose historic farm includes several listed buildings. The saddle in its name refers to the valley in which it lies. Its best-known feature is a treadmill, on which donkeys once plodded to draw up water.

Poynings: (pronounced *Punnins*) a small village with THE HOLY TRINITY CHURCH and THE ROYAL OAK (tel: 01273 857389).

The Devil's Dyke: a natural valley, but the legend (which has many variations) is that the Devil started to dig it, at night, to let in the sea and so drown the churches of the Weald. When an old lady was aroused by the noise and lit a lamp, the cocks started to crow, and the Devil fled in the belief that dawn had come. A little preliminary surveying would have saved a lot of trouble. Although not quite Britain's answer to the Grand Canyon, the dyke is an impressive hollow. Once there was a cable car, a railway link with Brighton, and a funicular railway above Poynings, all now mercifully gone.

The Clayton Windmills: Jack and Jill are of different types. JILL is a post mill – the whole structure was turned to face the wind. After a few hundred years somebody realised that only the cap need revolve, and tower mills like JACK were built. Tower mills are built of brick or stone; smock mills are of the same type but wooden. Open: JILL only, May – Sep, Sundays and bank hols.

Walk 21

Plumpton Plain, Balmer Down, Kingston near Lewes (L), Blackcap

Distances: out 13.0 km, 8.0 miles; return 11.5 km, 7.0 miles

Ascent: out 235m; return 265m

Times: out 3:20; return 3:05

Maps: Explorer 122, Landranger 198

Parking: Ditchling Beacon car park (NT), small charge, on minor road south of Ditchling (m/r 333130).

The walk: long, but one of the best. Mainly on high ridges with superb views.

Shorter walk: park at the junction of the B2116 and the lane to East Chiltington (m/r 372130), and walk up the escarpment to Blackcap.

---

1. From the car park, cross the road and follow the SDW E over **Streat Hill**. Cross the private road to Streathill Farm (1,900m) and continue over **Plumpton Plain** to gates (1,750m) and a NT Sign *Blackcap*. Turn sharply right just before the gates (this turn is often missed) and follow the SDW SW to join a track at a bend (1,100). Turn left, and follow the track downhill (SE) under power lines. Where it ends (650m) continue along a path along the edge of a field and over **Balmer Down** to a stile in an overgrown hedge (1,100m).

2. The SDW was diverted here so that the busy A27 could be crossed by a bridge. This walk follows the original route, which is shorter and more attractive. The map shows the diversion. Continue SE into a bottom (700m), bear right uphill to a wood (180m), and follow a path through it (200m) and round to the right. Keep left at a fork and walk down to the A27 (400m).

3. Cross and take a track between the Little Chef and a garage. Go under the railway (250m), keep right and follow a path SW up *Newmarket Hill*. At the top there are two gates (1,600m). Take the one on the left and continue gently uphill (ENE) above the impressive **Cold Coombes**. Go through another gate (300m) and continue over the brow of a hill to a track (100m). Bear left and continue along the main ridge. By two dew ponds (1,050m) follow the SDW round to the right. Continue ESE past a bostal on the left (650m) and, at a junction of tracks (180m), turn left down another bostal, and shortly (30m) take a path on the left. Go steeply downhill into woodland

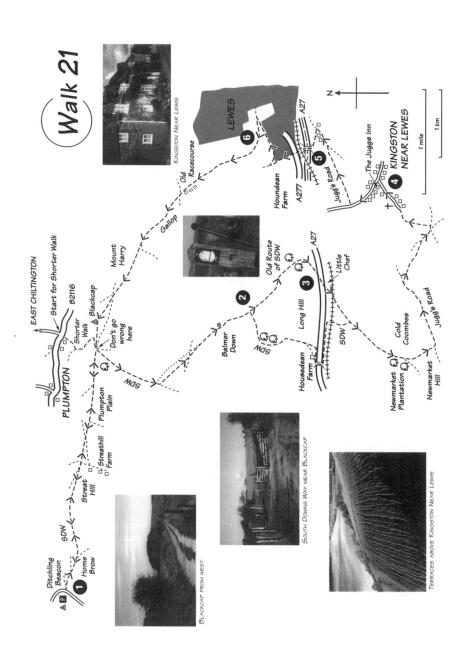

Walk 21

KINGSTON NEAR LEWES

LEWES

N

1 km
1 mile

6

A27

5

The Juggs Inn

4 KINGSTON
   NEAR LEWES

Old Racecourse

Houndean Farm

A27

Jugg's Road

Gallop

Mount Harry

2

Old Route of SDW

A27

3

Little Chef

Jugg's Road

EAST CHILTINGTON

Start for Shorter Walk

B2116

Shorter Walk

Blackcap

Don't go wrong here

Balmer Down

SDW

Long Hill

SDW

Cold Coombes

PLUMPTON

SDW

Plumpton Plain

Houseedean Farm

Newmarket Plantation

Newmarket Hill

Streathill Farm

Streat Hill

SDW

Ditchling Beacon

1 Home Brow

BLACKCAP FROM WEST

SOUTH DOWNS WAY NEAR BLACKCAP

TERRACES ABOVE KINGSTON NEAR LEWIS

and a stile at the bottom (550m). Turn right, join a road and continue past the church into **Kingston near Lewes** and the inn (550m).

4. **Return:** continue to the main road (70m), turn left and walk NW through the village and up a hill. At the top (550m) turn right along a private road with a sign *No Through Road, To Juggs Corner, Barn Acre & Tumblers Only*. Go ENE along **Jugg's Road** past houses to a ridge, where the road becomes a track, and continue between fields. Just before the first building on the right (1,200m) turn left through a kissing gate and go downhill across a field to its bottom corner (300m).

5. Cross the A27 by a farm bridge and go under the railway. Go uphill along a concrete track and cross the A277 (250m) on the outskirts of **Lewes**. Continue NNW along a track with a sign *Houndean Farm* and keep right just before the farm (350m). Turn sharply back to the right (100m) along a path going uphill. Follow the path round to the left and continue over a crossing path (400m) with houses on the right, until the path levels and meets a track (380m). Turn sharply back to the left along the track, which soon becomes a path, and swings to the right.

The church of St Pancras

6. Continue NW along the ridge to the equestrian centre sited on the
old Lewes Racecourse (1,500m). Walk past it (250) and continue
along a path, which later runs beside a training gallop, and follow it
onto the NT property at Blackcap. Continue past a path on the left
(1,000m) and go uphill along the flank of Mount Harry to the triangulation pillar on **Blackcap** (1,200m). Walk to the gate to join the
SDW and the outward route (400m) and follow the SDW W back to
the car park (3,650m).

En route

Newmarket Hill: at its foot, the LITTLE CHEF was formerly the
Newmarket Inn and may still be shown as *PH* on older maps. The garage
also sells refreshments. It is hard to believe that in 1997 the track up the
hill was dug up to lay a new water main; the restoration was excellent.

Kingston near Lewes: the CHURCH OF ST PANCRAS has a tapsell gate.
The JUGGS INN (tel: 01273 472523) is usually busy, and must be one of
the few inns which supplies a pager to indicate when food is ready.
JUGGS is the name of the flat baskets carried by the Brighton fishwives
who used the track to bring their husbands' catch to Lewes.

Walk 22

Standean Bottom, Highdole Hill, Rodmell (L), Balsdean Bottom

Distances: out 9.5 km, 6.0 miles; return 9.5 km, 6.0 miles

Ascent: out 140m; return 295m

Times: out 2:25; return 2:40

Maps: Explorer 122, Landranger 198

Parking: car park at high point on Falmer–Woodingdean road (m/r 356063).

The walk: explores two delightful bottoms which include old-style sheep-walks and, in Castle Hill National Nature Reserve, some unploughed downland.

Shorter walk: on the return, continue along the SDW instead of turning left to Balsdean Bottom.

---

1. Two tracks leave the car park. Take the one on the right, and follow it E towards a radio mast. Take a path on the left (600m) beside a fence, and follow it as it winds along the flank of **Bullock Hill**, whose name recalls the former use of oxen on the Downs. Go gently downhill and round to the right into **Standean Bottom**. Follow the path round a giant hairpin and beside a row of sycamores to a junction of tracks (2,800m).

2. Turn right and follow a track S along a bottom, then gently uphill. Where the track swings right (850m), turn sharply back left along a path and follow it ENE, downhill then up. At the top keep right along a track (550m) and continue past a ruined building and a memorial to John Harvey (a recent addition in 1999). At a fork by a second ruined building keep right (350m). Continue ESE past a footpath on the left (850m) and a track on the right (400m), then turn left (150m) along a footpath on the flank of **Highdole Hill**.

3. Continue below gorse bushes and bear slightly left (ENE) over **Fore Hill**. At a gate (1,300m) bear NE away from the fence towards a house prominent ahead, **Mill Hill** (also the name of the hill). At the bottom (500m) bear left and follow the edge of a field uphill and round to the right. At the top (400m) continue down a private road to ***Rodmell*** (850m).

4. **Return:** walk back up **Mill Hill**. At the top (850m) turn right along a path, the SDW, to the right of the house. Continue along a broad un-

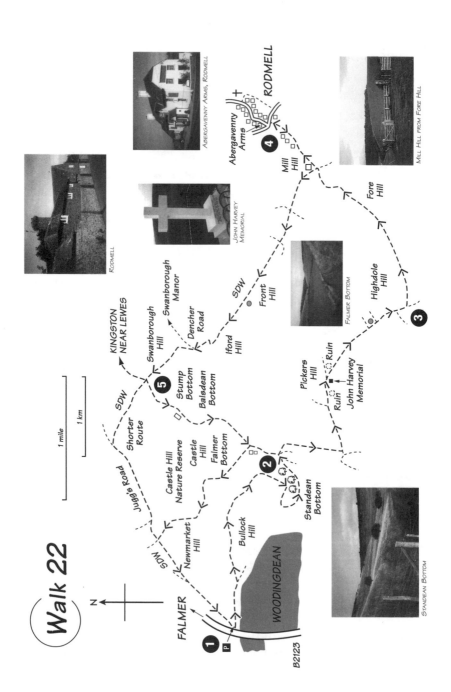

Walk 22

N

ABERGAVENNY ARMS, RODMELL

RODMELL

RODMELL

MILL HILL FROM FORE HILL

JOHN HARVEY MEMORIAL

Abergavenny Arms

Mill Hill

Fore Hill

Highdole Hill

FALMER BOTTOM

Front Hill

SDW

Swanborough Manor

Swanborough Hill

Dencher Road

Iford Hill

Ruin

Pickers Hill

Ruin

John Harvey Memorial

KINGSTON NEAR LEWES

SDW

Shorter Route

Jugg's Road

SDW

1 mile

1 km

Stump Bottom

Baladean Bottom

Castle Hill Nature Reserve

Castle Hill

Falmer Bottom

Newmarket Hill

Bullock Hill

WOODINGDEAN

Standean Bottom

STANDEAN BOTTOM

FALMER

P

B2123

dulating ridge and join a concrete track (1,050m) on **Front Hill**. Where this turns left (1,550m), turn right and then left (70m), and continue NW below the crest of the ridge. Pass **Dencher Road** (150m), a track down to Swanborough Manor on the right, and continue over Swanborough Hill to the next junction, above Kingston near Lewes (800m).

5. Follow the track round to the left, leaving the SDW, over a cattle grid and down (SW) into **Balsdean Bottom**. The track ends by a barn on the right (650m), which may not appear on the map. Bear left along the grassy bottom and then follow the RoW a little to the right of the lowest ground. (950m) Just before a group of buildings, some of them roofless, turn right and follow a path NW along the right-hand side of **Falmer Bottom**, going sharply left (750) and then more gently right. Continue past double metal gates (the map may show the RoW going through these) (300m), then take a small wooden gate on the right (160m). Follow a track NW through **Castle Hill,** a National Nature Reserve. Go steeply uphill, turn left at the top (600m) and follow a track SW back to the car park (1,500m).

En route

Rodmell: the village north of the main road repays exploration. The guide to ST PETER'S CHURCH makes the point that much-criticised Victorian restoration at least kept the building standing. There are many other old buildings, among them MONK'S HOUSE, the former home of Virginia Woolf (NT; open Apr-Oct, Wed & Sat, 2.00-5.00; tel: 01892 890651). The inn is THE ABERGAVENNY ARMS (tel: 01273 472416).

St Peter's Church, Rodmell

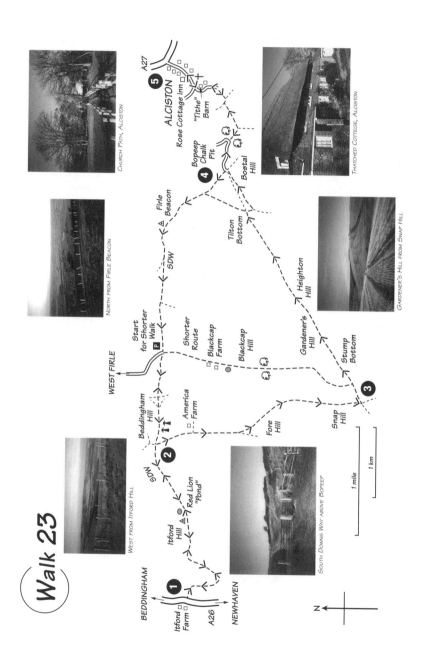

Walk 23

CHURCH PATH, ALCISTON

NORTH FROM FIRLE BEACON

THATCHED COTTAGE, ALCISTON

GARDENER'S HILL FROM SNAP HILL

WEST FROM ITFORD HILL

SOUTH DOWNS WAY ABOVE BOPEEP

ALCISTON

Rose Cottage Inn

"Tithe" Barn

Bopeep Chalk Pit

Bostal Hill

Firle Beacon

SDW

Tilton Bottom

Heighton Hill

Start for Shorter Walk

Shorter Route

Blackcap Farm

Blackcap Hill

Gardener's Hill

Stump Bottom

Snap Hill

WEST FIRLE

Beddingham Hill

America Farm

Fore Hill

SDW

Itford Hill

Red Lion

"Pond"

BEDDINGHAM

Itford Farm

A26

NEWHAVEN

A27

1 mile

1 km

N

Walk 23

Beddingham Hill, Heighton Hill, Alciston (L), Firle Beacon

Distances: out 12.0 km, 7.5 miles; return 9.0 km, 5.5 miles

Ascent: out 330m; return 195m

Times: out 3:15; return 2:20

Maps: Explorer 123, Landranger 198, 199

Parking: on A26 opposite Itford Farm (m/r 433055)

The walk: the brevity of the route description indicates its nature – a series of high ridges with fine views. On the outward route, ploughing and crops may make RoWs difficult to detect.

Shorter walks: 1. Start at the car park above West Firle (m/r 468058). Either go W to pick up the outward route on Beddingham Hill, or go south past Blackcap Farm to Stump Bottom. 2. If a pub lunch is not required, the descent to Alciston can be omitted.

---

1. Opposite **Itford Farm**, follow a track, the SDW, uphill, round to the right and then round to the left. Where it straightens and heads for a field (600m), keep left and follow a grassy path ENE along the flank of *Itford Hill*, soon with a fence on the right (which may not appear on the Explorer map). At the corner of a field bear right (550m) and continue past the triangulation pillar (600m) towards the radio towers.

2. About 250m before the towers, there are two sets of gates (1,100m). Turn right and go diagonally across a field (SE). Continue across the next and into another, passing the buildings of **America Farm** on the left (550m) (there is no farmhouse). In the next field, keep left at a fork (650m) and go SE, uphill along its edge. By a patch of scrub, bear a little to the right and continue over **Fore Hill**. Go downhill and then up, and in the next field bear slightly right and continue S over **Snap Hill**. Descend to a junction of paths by the corners of fields (1900m).

3. Turn left and follow a sunken path down (NE) to **Stump Bottom** (300m). Continue up **Gardener's Hill** and along the ridge to **Heighton Hill**. Bear slightly left to a gate (1,300m) and continue with a fence on the right to another gate. Cross a field, following a path which swings gently right and continue uphill, aiming for an old gate post and then a waymark post (1,500m). Here a RoW crosses – its visibility depends on the state of cultivation. Although a RoW goes straight on, it is often easier to turn right to a track (100m), then left to the Bopeep car park on **Bostal Hill** (650m) (see Walk 24).

4. Go down the lane to a hairpin bend (450m). Keep straight on SE through a gate on the right, and follow the left-hand of two paths, which contours the hillside. Go through a small wood, take a path on the left (200m) and follow it NE downhill to a track (500m). Turn right and then left at a junction of tracks (60m). Continue along a lane into *Alciston* and the inn (750m).

5. **Return:** walk back to the car park on Bostal Hill (1,960m), and turn right (NW) along the SDW to *Firle Beacon* (1150m). Follow the ridge round to the W and continue through the car park above Firle (1,700m). Continue past the radio towers on **Beddingham Hill** (1,100m) and rejoin the outward route at the gates (250m). Continue past the triangulation pillar on **Itford Hill** (1,100m) and begin the descent. Where the slope steepens bear left (600m) and continue beside a fence. On meeting a track (550m), turn right and follow it back to Itford Farm (600m).

Walkers above Alciston

En route

Itford Hill: the views between ITFORD HILL and BEDDINGHAM HILL are spectacular. RED LION POND by the trig point is now a dry grassy hollow.

Firle Beacon: one of the best summits on the Downs. Because of its height, 217m, and because it stands at a bend in the ridge, it gives fine views and is prominent in many others.

Alciston: (pronounced *Arlston*) is a quiet village (the road is a dead-end) with flint and thatched houses. It has a famous XIV century TITHE BARN, 56m long, still very much in use. In spite of its name, it was built for normal agricultural purposes. Alciston Church (dedication unknown) is Norman, but restored in the XIX century. Nearby is a ruined mediaeval dovecote. The ROSE COTTAGE INN (tel: 01323 870377) is a fine old hostelry with a collection of bank notes in the bar. Its unusual name is because it started life as a private house. The sign is not missing, it's on the A27.

Walk 24

High and Over, Seaford Head, Exceat (L), Alfriston

Distances: out 11.5 km 7.5 miles; return 9.0 km 5.5 miles

Ascent: out 45m; return 190m

Times: out 2:40; return 2:20

Maps: Explorer 123, Landranger 198, 199

Parking: the lane to *Bopeep* Bostal car park (m/r 493050) is signposted only as a by-way. It leaves the A27 just south of Selmeston.

The walk: another of my favourites. It includes two classic views – the Cuckmere River from High and Over and the Seven Sisters from Seaford Head. A pleasant ridge over Norton Top and the valley of the Cuckmere are also explored.

Shorter walks: 1. From High and Over, descend NE and join the return route. 2. Return from Exceat Bridge.

Caution: the paths beside the Cuckmere River are muddy and slippery after rain, and in severe weather may be impassable due to flooding.

---

1. The SDW passes the car park. Take a track at right angles to it and follow it SW and round to the left past the triangulation pillar on **Norton Top** (1,950m). At a junction of tracks and paths (950m), where there is a seat in memory of *Paul Earl*, take the left-hand of two tracks and follow it S and gently round to the left, with a golf course on the right. Pass a NT sign *Frog Firle* (1,300m) and bear left into a field (100m). Follow its edge E past a gate on the left to a road and turn right (1,250m)

2. Cross the road (50m) and cross the car park on **High and Over** to a gravelled path. Follow this SE to a view indicator and continue steeply downhill along a grassy path towards the river. At the bottom (500m), cross a plank bridge and a footbridge, then turn right (SW) along the embankment (250m), parts of which require care in the wet. Just before a fence (1,250m), bear right and turn left along the A259 to **Exceat Bridge** and the inn (200m).

3. Cross the road and walk through the pub car park. Take a path with a NT sign *Chyngton Farm*. At the entrance to **Seaford Head Nature Reserve** (320m) turn left and follow the path round to the right beside the river (if muddy keep straight on along the return route – the going is much better) and continue almost to the sea (1,250m). Turn

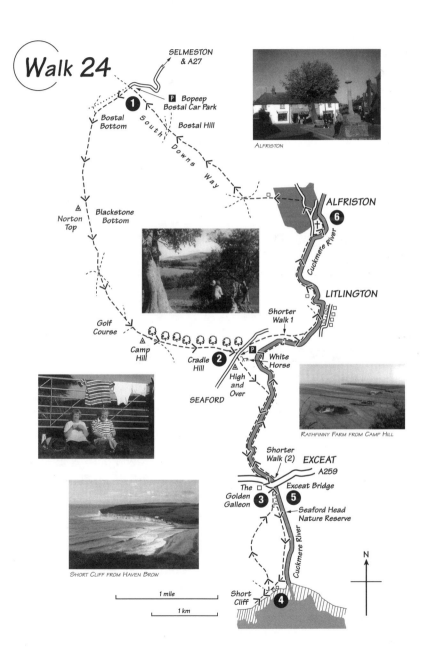

Walk 24

SELMESTON
& A27

P Bopeep
Bostal Car Park
1

Bostal
Bottom

South

Bostal Hill

Downs

Way

ALFRISTON

ALFRISTON
6

Norton
Top

Blackstone
Bottom

Cuckmere River

LITLINGTON

Golf
Course

Shorter
Walk 1

Camp
Hill

Cradle
Hill
2

P

White
Horse

High
and
Over

SEAFORD

RATHFINNY FARM FROM CAMP HILL

Shorter
Walk (2)

EXCEAT
A259

The
Golden
Galleon
3

Exceat Bridge
5

Seaford Head
Nature Reserve

Cuckmere River

N

SHORT CLIFF FROM HAVEN BROW

1 mile

1 km

Short
Cliff
4

right on shingle and climb a track past cottages (150m). Bear left along a grassy path to **Short Cliff**. It is not necessary to climb very far up **Seaford Head** for the classic view of The Seven Sisters (200m allowed in distances).

High and Over: a view of the White Horse

4. Return to the track just above the cottages (200m+) and take a path on the left. Follow it to join another (150m) and continue along the foot of the hill back to *Exceat Bridge* (1,650m) and the inn.

5. **Return:** cross the river, turn left and follow a path N along its east bank. Continue below the White Horse and cross a farm bridge (New Bridge) (2,600m). Turn right, and follow the west bank to the footbridge to **Litlington** (700m) (see Walk 25) but do not cross. Keep right at a path junction and continue along the west bank to **Alfriston** (see Walk 26).

6. Continue past the footbridge (1,700m). Just before a gate and stile (100m) turn left and follow a track and a lane to the main road (120m). Turn right and immediately keep left past Ye Olde Smugglers Inne. Continue to **North Road** (280m) and turn left (W) towards the escarpment. Where the road ends, continue steeply uphill along a track which shrinks to a path. Join a track (800m) and at the top (100m) turn right along another track, which is the SDW. Continue NW over **Bostal Hill** to the car park (2,350m).

En route

Bopeep: the name is a reference to a turn-pike keeper who watched avidly for travellers on the future A27.

High and Over: there are superb views over the Cuckmere River, best seen from a point below the view indicator. The White Horse on the eastern slope is XIX century. The terraces were created to facilitate ploughing.

Exceat: the GOLDEN GALLEON (tel: 01323 892247) offers good food and has its own brewery. There is a restaurant by the VISITOR CENTRE, 500m along the A259 (see Walk 25).

Walk 25

Exceat, Seven Sisters, Birling Gap (L), Friston Forest

Distances: out 8.5 km, 5.5 miles; return 8.0 km, 5.0 miles

Ascent: out 395m; return 220m

Times: out 2:40; return 2:10

Maps: Explorer 123, Landranger 199

Parking: in Litlington is not encouraged. There are spaces along the lane just south of the village.

The walk: a great favourite. The traverse of the Seven Sisters, with their superb chalk cliffs, is one of the highlights of walking the Downs. The walk includes more ascent than any other in this book.

Shorter walk: start at Exceat, where there are two car parks (charge made), and return through Friston Forest. Better still, do the Seven Sisters in both directions.

---

1. The outward route follows the footpath section of the SDW, and the initial section is waymarked for *Westdean*. From the bend in the lane, walk up a private road beside the village hall, and very shortly take a path on the right (35m). Continue S over a hill and down into **Charleston Bottom** (950m). Turn left along a path, and where it swings left, take steps on the right (100m) and go uphill (S) into Friston Forest, where the path becomes a track. At the top of the hill pass another track on the left (350m), follow the track round to the left, and pass a path on the right (130m). Continue ESE along a path which contours the hillside, and at a T-junction turn right (400m) and descend to *Westdean*.

2. Join a lane (160m), at which point a detour to the left may be made to visit the church and the old parsonage (see map). By an attractive pond (100m), follow steps steeply uphill through woodland (SW). At the top (220m) there is a superb view over the Cuckmere River (the climb can be avoided by a detour to the right – see map). Go down to the Visitor Centre at *Exceat* (180m).

3. The SDW used to run beside the river, but was diverted to the east. Cross the road to a concrete track and immediately take a grassy path on the left (some ascent may be avoided by following the concrete track). Follow a path round to the right (SE) above the track. The stone on the site of the vanished church is best found by continuing to the first fence (800m) and looking back to the left – the top of

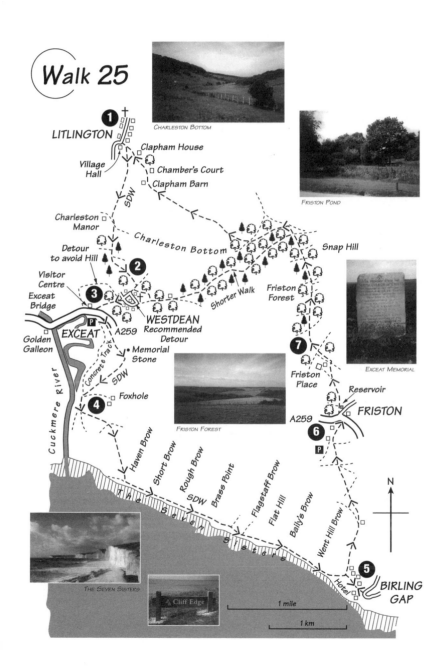

Walk 25

CHARLESTON BOTTOM

FRISTON POND

EXCEAT MEMORIAL

FRISTON FOREST

THE SEVEN SISTERS

Cliff Edge

1 mile

1 km

the stone can be seen at the highest point. From the fence, bear right and follow waymark posts SW down to the concrete track (650m).

Cross it and follow a track towards the sea. Take a path on the left (100m), climb a short flight of stone steps (90m) and bear left uphill (ESE) with a fence on the right (the fence runs beside the SDW, and is not shown on the 1999 Explorer map). Follow the fence round to the right and cross a stile (900m) – this is Haven Brow, the first of the *Seven Sisters*. Bear left and follow the magnificent switchback to a kissing gate (2,950m) above *Birling Gap*. Go the left of a fence and turn right along a path (100m). Follow a track between houses to the car pack and hotel (300m).

5. **Return:** walk back past the houses (300m) to a gate. Turn right and follow a path past Seven Sisters Cottage, and go N up **Went Hill**. Just past a red-roofed barn, where the more obvious path swings left (700m) keep straight on along the ridge to a gate (400m). The next section of the route, although widely used, is not shown on current (1999) OS maps. Continue WNW across a field aiming for a kissing gate (350m), cross another field to a track by houses (260m), and turn right to the A259 and **Friston** (300m) (see Walk 28)

6. Cross the A259 and a grass triangle, and follow a path downhill into a wood. Keep right by a reservoir and descend to a field (220m). Cross this WNW to a private road to **Friston Place** (250m), cross another field to another private road (220m), and turn left along a path which runs beside it. Where the road swings left (200m) keep straight on across a track into woodland and immediately follow a path round to the right. Continue uphill and cross a stretch of downland into **Friston Forest** (300m).

7. Continue N along a grassy ride. Go downhill, cross a made track (450m) and continue over **Snap Hill**. Descend, cross a bridleway (750m), and go downhill and round to the left. At the next junction (200m) turn left (WSW) along a crossing track, signposted *Charleston Bottom*. Descend, cross the bottom (400m) and continue W uphill along a track opposite. Continue to the edge of the forest (200m) and follow a path, which soon becomes a track, WNW through fields. At **Clapham Barn** (1,300m) bear right and pass the farm buildings on the left. Just before a house (100m), keep left at a fork. Continue to a lane and follow it back to the start (550m).

En route

Litlington: a charming little village. The dedication of the NORMAN CHURCH is unknown. The LITLINGTON TEA GARDENS are the oldest in Sussex (open Apr – Oct; tel: 01323 870222), and the inn is the PLOUGH AND HARROW.

Westdean: the flint buildings are superb – do make the detour to see the CHURCH OF ALL SAINTS and THE OLD PARSONAGE. Except for the church, all the buildings are private.

Exceat: (pronounced *Exeet*) the village has gone, a victim of the Black Death and French raids (see route description for the memorial stone on the site of the old church). THE SEVEN SISTERS COUNTRY PARK VISITOR CENTRE occupies a fine old barn and has interesting displays, a shop, and public toilets. There is also the EXCEAT FARMHOUSE LICENSED RESTAURANT (tel: 01323 870218) and an inn at EXCEAT BRIDGE (Walk 24).

The Seven Sisters: accuracy has been sacrificed to alliteration – there are really eight, the uncounted one being little FLAT HILL, between FLAGSTAFF BROW and BAILY'S BROW. It is always worth remembering that this area could have been covered by bungalows.

Seaford Head and The Seven Sisters

Birling Gap: not the most attractive spot on the Downs, but one of the most popular. There are the BIRLING GAP HOTEL AND COFFEE SHOP (tel: 01323 423197), public toilets, and steps down to the foreshore. Some of the cottages have toppled into the sea as the cliffs are eroded. Late in 1999, planning permission was granted for a sea wall to protect the cottages, to the annoyance of those who believe that nature should be allowed to take its course.

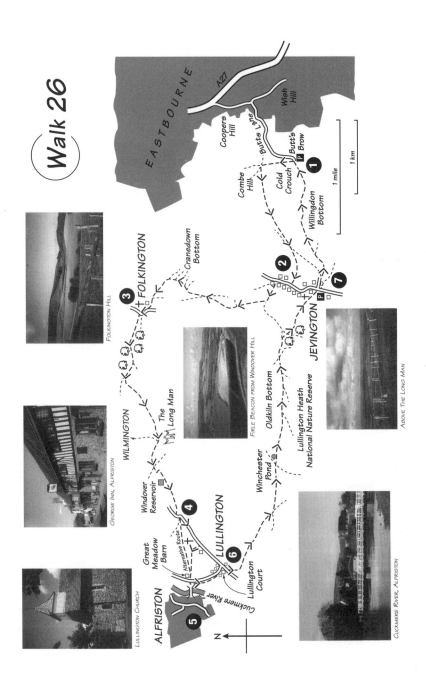

Walk 26

EASTBOURNE

A27

Coopers Hill

Wish Hill

Butt's Brow

Butt's Lane

1

Cold Crouch

Combe Hill

Willingdon Bottom

1 km

1 mile

2

7

Cranedown Bottom

FOLKINGTON

3

JEVINGTON

FIRLE BEACON FROM WINDOVER HILL

Oldkiln Bottom

ABOVE THE LONG MAN

FOLKINGTON HILL

WILMINGTON

The Long Man

Lullington Heath National Nature Reserve

Windover Reservoir

Winchester Pond

GEORGE INN, ALFRISTON

Great Meadow Barn

4

Alternative Route

LULLINGTON

6

Lullington Court

Cuckmere River

ALFRISTON

5

N

LULLINGTON CHURCH

CUCKMERE RIVER, ALFRISTON

Walk 26

Jevington, Folkington, Alfriston (L), Lullington Heath

Distances: out 9.0 km, 5.5 miles; return 7.0 km, 4.5 miles

Ascent: out 100m; return 275m

Times: out 2:10; return 2:05

Maps: Explorer 123, Landranger 199

Parking: a free car park at Butt's Brow (m/r 579017) is not signposted. From the A22 in Eastbourne take a minor road through Willingdon, named Cooper's Hill (N) and Wish Hill (S). Turn up Butts Lane to the car park, which is very popular with Eastbourne's dog-owners.

The walk: one of the shorter ones, leaving time for to explore Alfriston. The return crosses some fine country but involves three stiff ascents.

Shorter walk: start at Jevington, where there is a car park (m/r 561012).

---

1. There are parking areas on either side at the top of **Butts Lane.** Just inside the lower one, take a kissing gate, and follow a path N over Cold Crouch to a barrow on the summit of **Combe Hill** (650m). Both summits can be by-passed on the left. Follow the path round to the left and continue along the ridge. Go down through scrub to a path (450m) and follow it SW across a field. Keep right at a fork (600m) and continue to a path between fences (350m). Continue to a road (220m) and The Eight Bells at **Jevington** (see Walk 27).

2. Turn right and take Green Lane (a track) on the left (220m). Go WNW past a path on the right (80m) and take the next path on the right (220m) (where the Wealdway sign was indicating the wrong direction in 1999) and follow it NNW between overgrown hedges. By **Cranedown Bottom** (1,050m), which can be visited by a path not shown on the map, the Polegate Windmill can be seen on the right. The path swings left by a reservoir and crosses a field, then runs WNW along its foot. At the top of a rise there is a lane and the tiny hamlet of *Folkington* (1,000m).

3. Continue along a track, signposted *Public Byway Wilmington.* Go uphill and pass a public bridleway on the left (600m) (which may not be shown as a RoW on the map). At the end of a hanger (200m) take a gate on the left with a sign *Folkington Estate Public Bridleway.* Follow a path SW along the base of the escarpment above **Wilmington** (see Walk 28) and below the Long Man (950m). Con-

tinue over a crossing path (400m) to a fence (110m). Turn left and then right (35m) along a track, which is the SDW. Follow the track WSW past **Windover Reservoir** to a lane (650m).

4. Turn left along the lane and take a brick path on the right (450m), which begins at a cottage and is signposted *Public Footpath to Lullington Church.* The church at **Lullington** can be visited by a detour to the right. The road can be avoided by the paths shown on the map. Continue W along the edge of a field to a road (500m) and **Great Meadow Barn** (formerly Plonk Barn – why change the name?). Cross to a path and follow it over the Cuckmere River into **Alfriston** (300m).

5. **Return:** take the outward path (by the United Reformed Church) and walk back towards **Great Meadow Barn.** Just before the road take a path on the right (300m) which runs beside it. Continue to a stile at **Lullington** (300m) and join the road. At a T-junction (200m) turn right, and just past Lullington Court take a track on the left (130m), signposted *Jevington.*

6. Go uphill (ESE), turn half-left along a crossing track (1,050m) and continue E to a National Nature Reserve sign on the ridge and onto **Lullington Heath** (600m). Continue over a crossing track, go down into **Oddkiln Bottom** and continue uphill (E). Go over the crest of the ridge and a crossing track (1,400m) and follow a path, the SDW, downhill. At a fork (300m) keep right and continue SE down to St Andrew's church at **Jevington** (650). Follow a lane to a road (200m) and turn right and immediately (10m) left along Willingdon Lane.

7. At the end of the lane (150m) continue along a path, just above the bottom of a field. Follow it round to the left and gently uphill into a strip of woodland, past a path on the left (200m). Continue ENE along **Willingdon Bottom**, and uphill to the car park (1,450m).

En route

Folkington: THE MANOR, although its design is Tudor, was built in the XIX century. Beside it is ST PETER'S CHURCH and little else.

Lullington: was made famous by the late Dirk Bogarde's book about his childhood, *Great Meadow.* The CHURCH, one of the smallest in the country, is the chancel of a larger building which was destroyed at an uncertain date.

Alfriston: (pronounced *All-friston*) a beautiful old village and popular tourist centre. The CHURCH OF ST ANDREW is sometimes referred to as the "Cathedral of the Downs" – it is big, but not that big. Unlike most churches in the Downs, it was all built at the same time. Nearby is THE CLERGY HOUSE, the first property owned by The National Trust (open 27 Mar – 31 Oct, except Tue and Fri, 1000 – 1630; tel: 01323 870001). The HERITAGE CENTRE is no longer open. There are shops and many places to eat and drink. My own favourite is the bar of THE WINGROVE INN (tel: 01323 870276), which has jazz on Sundays and is one of the friendliest pubs in Sussex.

St Andrew's church, Alfriston

Lullington Heath: is very unusual. Heathland usually occurs on acidic soils; this National Nature Reserve is a rare example of heathland on al-kaline chalk. A brochure is available (sometimes) at a sign in Oddkiln Bottom.

Walk 27

Beachy Head, Willingdon Hill, Jevington (L)

Distances: out 11.5 km, 7.0 miles; return 9.5 km, 6.0 miles

Ascent: out 270m; return 165m

Times: out 3:00; return 2:25

Maps: Explorer 123, Landranger 199

Parking: large car park at Birling Gap (m/r 554960) (see Walk 25)

The walk: long uninterrupted stretches over downland ridges and by coastal cliffs are the outstanding feature of this walk.

Shorter walk: from Willingdon Hill, follow the return route, omitting Jevington (and the lunch stop).

---

1. Take a path by a telephone box and follow it SE, close to the cliff edge. There are fine retrospective views of the Seven Sisters. Go inland of **Belle Tout** (1,050m) and continue along the cliff top to **Beachy Head** (2,800m to the triangulation pillar).

2. From the buildings, follow a path round with the road on the left. It is soon possible to move away from the road and its traffic and follow a path N, parallel to it. Continue to a road junction (1,900m) and cross the larger road, the B2103. Follow a grassy path signposted *Jevington* and *Wilmington* which bears WNW away from the road. Continue above a hanger to a prominent seat on the skyline. Continue past a dewpond and a triangulation pillar (650m) to the A259 (500m) and cross by the golf clubhouse.

3. From this point there is often a choice of two or even three paths or tracks. Continue WNW though the golf course and then by a field on the left. Bear round to the left to the triangulation pillar on **Willingdon Hill** (2,350m) and bear left again NW, downhill towards Jevington, which is in sight. Where the track divides (170m) keep right. Cross a stile on the right (400m) and follow a path WNW through a field towards the village. At the bottom (550m) turn left along a path beside a fence, not the more obvious track. Continue through trees, bear right in a field to a lane (350m) (Willingdon Lane) and follow it into *Jevington* (150m). At a T-junction turn right and walk to the inn (380m).

4. **Return:** from the inn turn right, walk back past Willingdon Lane

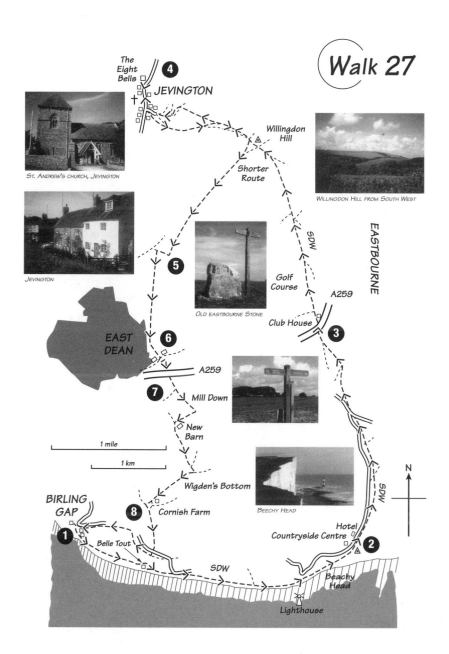

The Eight Bells

4

JEVINGTON

St. Andrew's church, Jevington

Jevington

Walk 27

Willingdon Hill

Shorter Route

Willingdon Hill from South West

5

Old eastbourne Stone

Golf Course

SDW

A259

Club House

3

EASTBOURNE

EAST DEAN

6

A259

7 Mill Down

New Barn

1 mile

1 km

Wigden's Bottom

BIRLING GAP

8 Cornish Farm

Beechy Head

Hotel

Countryside Centre

2

1

Belle Tout

SDW

N

SDW

Lighthouse

Beachy Head

(370m), and shortly turn left along Eastbourne Lane (35m). Continue along a track and follow it E, up onto **Willingdon Hill**. Just before the summit with its stone, turn right (1,450m) and follow a track SW, just below the crest of the ridge. Move left to a wooden gate (190m) and follow a path along the crest of the ridge. Rejoin the track (250m) and where it ends by old buildings continue along a grassy path. Belle Tout is prominent on the left.

5. Continue SW and, just before a metal gate (1,350m), turn right along the edge of a field. At the corner of a field on the left (160m) turn left through a small wooden gate. Follow the edge of a field downhill (S) to the corner of a housing estate at **East Dean** (800m), where there are two gates and a stile. Take the gate on the left and follow a path along the edge of a field beside the houses, down and round to the left to a metalled track (600m).

6. Cross the track to a small wooden gate and turn right along a grassy path (a signpost indicates an impassable route straight ahead). Take another small wooden gate on the left (40m) and double back along the bottom of a field. Just past the first gate (35m), bear right steeply uphill along a grassy path (a signpost points in the wrong direction again), then, before reaching the edge of the field, make a right turn (80m). The tendency is to go too far to the left. Continue uphill to the A259 (180m).

7. Cross and follow a track, signposted *Cornish Farm*, SE over the ridge of **Mill Down**. Just before a metal gate (600m) turn right towards New Barn, just before which there is an old shepherd's cottage. Keep well to the right of the buildings (300m) to a small wooden gate, and bear left downhill (SE) to **Wigden's Bottom** (650m). Turn right along a track and follow it WSW past **Cornish Farm** (there is no farmhouse).

8. Follow a concrete track round to the left through a metal gate (650m) and immediately turn right along the edge of a field (the RoW runs beside, not along the obvious grassy track). At a corner (70m) turn left, and follow the edge of a field to rejoin the concrete track and follow it S to the road below **Belle Tout** (600m). Cross, ascend to a path (50m), turn right and follow the path back to **Birling Gap** (1,100m).

En route

Belle Tout: (pronounced too) the area used to see many shipwrecks.

The building was a lighthouse, but it was too often obscured by mist, and is now a private residence. In 1999 it was moved bodily away from the cliff edge, at great expense, to delay its fall into the encroaching sea.

Beachy Head

Beachy Head: is the highest chalk cliff in Britain. It was known to the Normans as *beau chef* – beautiful head – later corrupted to Beachy. There is a hotel, a coffee shop, a telescope, car parks and public toilets (in the main car park) – and of course the famous lighthouse. Ice cream is usually on sale. The COUNTRY CENTRE is well worth a visit. A very popular spot, which also has the unfortunate reputation as the country's favourite place for suicide.

Willingdon Hill: the stone, inscribed *Old Town Eastbourne* is not very ancient. It is from the bombed remains of Barclay's Bank in the town.

Jevington: ST ANDREW'S CHURCH has Saxon components, including its tower, which was probably used as a defence against Viking raids. As well as THE EIGHT BELLS, there are the JEVINGTON TEA GARDENS (tel: 01323 484745). THE HUNGRY MONK RESTAURANT opens for lunch on Sundays only (tel: 01323 482178).

Walk 28

Wilmington, Windover Hill, East Dean (L), Chapman's Bottom

Distances: out 9.5 km, 6.0 miles; return 11.0 km, 7.0 miles

Ascent: out 300m; return 245m

Times: out: 2:40; return: 2:55

Maps: Explorer 123, Landranger 199

Parking: car park at Wilmington, by the Priory (m/r 543041); height restriction 6ft 10in; public toilets.

The walk: one of the best, with high ridges giving superb views, quiet bottoms and broad-leaved forests.

Shorter walk: in Friston Forest, instead of turning right to Charleston Bottom, keep straight on over Snap Hill to Friston Place.

---

1. From the car park at **Wilmington**, cross the road and turn right along a path beside it. Leave the road (200m) and follow a path towards the Long Man. Turn left below the figure (550m) and follow a path along the flank of the hill. Turn sharply back right along a grassy path (a permissive bridleway) and make an ascending traverse of the hill. At a gate at the top, cross a stretch of pathless downland towards a fence (70m), and turn left along a path, the SDW. Continue round to the right above the impressive hollow of Deep Dean (Dene?) and at a fork keep right (250m).

2. Continue into a field (700m) and to a sign **Lullington Heath National Nature Reserve** (470m) (see Walk 26). Follow a track to a junction (280m) where there is another Nature Reserve Sign. Turn left and take a track just right of the sign which immediately swings right, and is waymarked *Charleston Bottom*. Continue downhill through **Friston Forest** to a junction of paths and tracks in a bottom (1,300m).

3. Turn right and follow a grassy path along **Charleston Bottom** into fields (600m). By a zigzag in the fence on the right (500m), keep to the left of a cattle trough and shortly turn sharply back to the left (110m). Follow a grassy path which climbs the flank of the hill and swings right to a gate (500m). The obvious short-cut is not a RoW. Take a gate on the right into **Friston Forest** and follow a broad grassy track. Continue along a made track (220m), keep left where a grassy

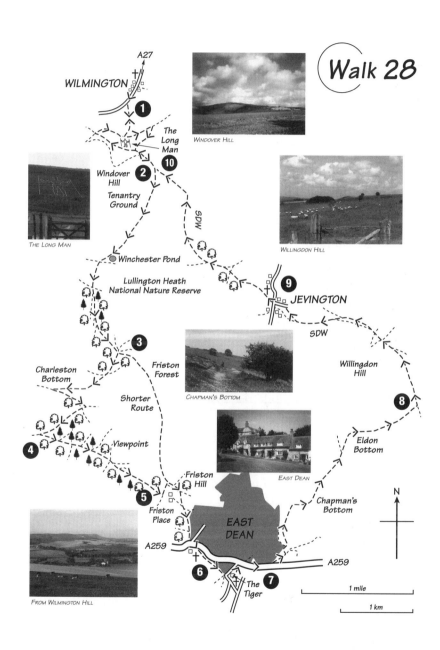

A27

WILMINGTON

1

WINDOVER HILL

The
Long
Man

10

THE LONG MAN

Windover
Hill

2

Tenantry
Ground

SDW

WILLINGDON HILL

Winchester Pond

Lullington Heath
National Nature Reserve

9 JEVINGTON

Charleston
Bottom

3

Friston
Forest

SDW

CHAPMAN'S BOTTOM

Willingdon
Hill

Shorter
Route

8

4

Viewpoint

EAST DEAN

Eldon
Bottom

Friston
Hill

5

Chapman's
Bottom

Friston
Place

EAST
DEAN

N

A259

FROM WILMINGTON HILL

6

A259

7

The
Tiger

1 mile

1 km

track goes off right (300m) and follow the track round to the left (this section may not be shown on the map). Turn left (120m) along another made track.

4. Continue through the forest. A sign at the top of a rise indicates a viewpoint on the left, but the view is restricted and not really worth the detour. Where the made track swings left (600m) keep straight on downhill. Cross a track at the bottom (250m) and continue along a track, which soon begins to climb **Friston Hill**. At the top, as the water tower comes into view, continue along the edge of downland, go downhill through woodland to a drive by **Friston Place** (800m) and turn left. Only glimpses of the house are possible through the hedge and trees.

5. Follow the drive round to the right (180m) and take a path which runs beside it on the left. Where the path ends (200m), cross the road and follow a faint path uphill across a field. Cross a private road (220m) and cross another field (250m) uphill to its far corner. Continue through woodland to the A295 (220m) at *Friston*, cross to the church and turn left. By a *No Overtaking* sign turn right (100m) into the graveyard and walk to its corner. Turn left and follow a path downhill to a NT sign *Crowlink*. Continue downhill through a field, which in early summer is ablaze with buttercups, to a road (500m) and follow it into *East Dean* (100m).

6. **Return:** from The Tiger, turn left and follow a wall round to the left along the edge of a car park. Follow a path beside the wall and then between houses to the A259 (220m), where there is a garage that sells snacks and drinks. Turn right along the main road and then left along Downsview Lane (350m).

7. Take The Laines on the left (350m), and at a T-junction continue along a path. At a junction (100m) turn right and continue to a field. Walk to a stile (100m), turn left just before it, and follow a fence round to the right into **Chapman's Bottom**. Cross a stile (700m) and continue along the bottom, now with a fence on the left, and cross another stile (950m). A path goes off left (45m) which may not be shown on the map. Keep right and follow the path round to the right into **Eldon Bottom**. Cross a stile (550m) and climb out of the bottom along the edge of a field. At the top turn left along a track (600m), which is the SDW.

8. Follow the track past the triangulation pillar on **Willingdon Hill**

(1,000m) (see Walk 27). Continue over a crossing track and bear round to the left and downhill towards Jevington. The track splits (170m) and re-unites (500m). Continue between trees to a stile on the right (550m). Cross, descend through a field to a lane at *Jevington* (see Walk 27) and continue to a road (300m).

9. Turn right and almost immediately left (10m) along Church Lane. Walk up to the church (200m) and continue along a path. Follow this uphill into woodland, bear right and continue over a crossing path (600m). Continue uphill as a path joins from the right (80m). At the edge of the wood, turn right (300m) and continue through a gate (450m). The traverse of the next section in evening sunlight is one of the great experiences of walking the South Downs. Follow a faint path in a gentle curve right and then left, following waymark posts, and rejoin the outward route above **Deep Dean** (1,050m).

10. About 50m before a gate on the skyline (250m) bear right to a stile (70m) (not a gate). Go downhill beside a fence on the right, take a gate on the right (650m) and follow a path to a gate below the Long Man (400m). Turn left, follow a path to the road (550m) and turn right back to the car park (120m).

The Tiger, East Dean

En route

Wilmington: the LONG MAN, 70 metres high on the hill to the north, is the largest representation of the human form in Europe. It is elongated, but appears correctly proportioned when seen from below. Its origins are unknown. There is also the CHURCH OF ST MARY & ST PETER, the ruins of WILMINGTON PRIORY (not open to the public) and the old pound. The church was shared by the monks of the priory, which was small, and the people of the village. The GIANT'S REST inn is on the lane near the main road.

Friston: there is no village. The CHURCH OF ST MARY THE VIRGIN is beautifully situated by a pond. The guide, written by the vicar who held the living from 1908 to 1929, informs the visitor that "windmills ... are rapidly vanishing; steam is cheaper". FRISTON FOREST covers over 2,000 acres, and consists mainly of broad-leaved trees. FRISTON PLACE is a Tudor manor house, not open to the public.

East Dean: a beautiful village green is surrounded by flint cottages and the XVI century TIGER INN (tel: 01323 423209). The oldest part of the CHURCH OF ST SIMON & ST JUDE is the Saxon tower, which was used for defence in the Saxon period. There are also the GRIMALDI RESTAURANT (tel: 01323 422384) and a VILLAGE STORES. The buildings north of the A259 are mainly modern.

Walk 29

Woodingdean, Ovingdean, Rottingdean

Distance: 12.0 km, 7.5 miles

Ascent: 230m

Time: 3:05

Maps: Explorer 122, Landranger 198

Parking: car park at high point on Falmer – Woodingdean road (m/r 356063), just north of urban sprawl

The walk: not the best in the book – the coastal towns are too much in evidence – but there are some pleasant parts. Rottingdean is well worth a visit, and is the only place on the walk where refreshment can be obtained.

---

1. From the car park, cross the road and follow a track SW above the houses of **Woodingdean**. Pass the last house and, at the corner of a field (1,350m), take a path on the left. Cross a road by a sign *Woodingdean* and turn left beside **Brighton Race Course** (130m). Join a track and follow the rails round to the right, then bear left (SE) away from them (300m), with a golf course on the right. The two large buildings ahead are St Dunstan's on the left and Roedean School on the right. Continue ESE to the end of the golf course (1,550m), go a little way uphill, turn sharply right and almost immediately (15m) keep left at a fork.

2. Follow a track up the flank of Cattle Hill and round to the left (180m), and continue S along a path with a fence on the left. Take a stile on the left (450m) and follow a path E, up **Cattle Hill** (for a closer view of Roedean, see the alternative route on the map). Go over the summit and turn right just before a stile (380m). Follow the edge of a field SSE and at its corner turn left (230m) and continue ESE with a fence on the right. Resist the temptation to peer into a brick tower – it is a vent for the Brighton sewer. Cross a stile on the right (400m) and continue down to a road, Greenways, at **Ovingdean** (250m).

3. Cross and ascend the road opposite, **Beacon Hill** (also the name of the hill). At the top (300m) take the right-hand of two paths and follow it SSE along the ridge. Continue past the *Beacon Hill Windmill* to a track between houses (1,000m). Turn left along a private road and descend to *Rottingdean* (200m).

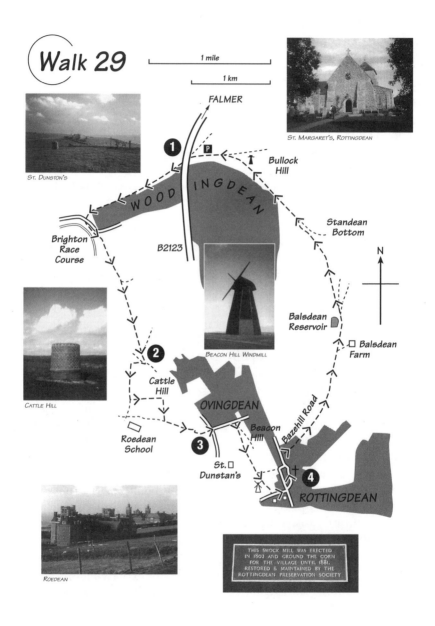

Walk 29

1 mile

1 km

FALMER

ST. DUNSTON'S

ST. MARGARET'S, ROTTINGDEAN

W O O D I N G D E A N

Bullock Hill

Standean Bottom

N

Brighton Race Course

B2123

Balsdean Reservoir

Balsdean Farm

CATTLE HILL

Cattle Hill

OVINGDEAN

Roedean School

Beacon Hill

Pazehill Road

St. Dunstan's

ROTTINGDEAN

BEACON HILL WINDMILL

ROEDEAN

THIS SMOCK MILL WAS ERECTED IN 1802 AND GROUND THE CORN FOR THE VILLAGE UNTIL 1881, RESTORED & MAINTAINED BY THE ROTTINGDEAN PRESERVATION SOCIETY

4. Turn left, take the first right and follow the road N through the village, against the one-way traffic flow, past the church and the pond. Turn right up **Bazehill Road** (450m) and follow it NE, up onto the downs. Continue along a private road (600m), past **Balsdean Farm** (850m) and over the brow of High Hill. Just past **Balsdean Reservoir** take a gate on the left at the corner of a field (450m), and follow a grassy track NNW, past a waymark post, to the far side. Continue along the edge of the next field to a junction above Standean Bottom (1,250m) and take a gate on the left. Continue NW between fences, then past the houses of **Woodingdean** and the radio tower, back to the start (1,700m).

En route

The Beacon Hill Windmill: is a smock mill. Its dark colour and stumpy sails give it a spectral air. Hilaire Belloc was responsible for its restoration in the 1920s.

Rottingdean: repays detailed exploration – there is an attractive pond and many lovely old buildings. One of the finest, TUDOR COURT, is strictly private, but there is a good view from the back of the churchyard. During the Hundred Years War, many villagers were burnt to death in the tower of ST MARGARET'S CHURCH during a French raid. The inexpensive guide to the church and village, for once not obsessed with architectural detail, is excellent value. There are inns, restaurants and shops, and a walk along the foot of the cliffs. ROTTINGDEAN GRANGE Museum contains a collection of

St Margaret's, Rottingdean

toys and memorabilia of Rudyard Kipling, who lived here until driven out by gawping trippers (open daily 10.00-16.00 except Weds, Sun 14.00-16.00; tel: 01273 301004).

Walk 30

Southease, Telscombe, Piddinghoe

Distance: 13 km, 8.0 miles

Ascent: 240m

Time: 3:20

Maps: Explorer 122, Landranger 198

Parking: just east of the bridge over the Ouse between Southease village and the railway station (m/r 428053). By car, approach from Southease – there is no public vehicular access from Itford Farm. Another option is to park by Itford Farm on the A26 (see Walk 23).

The walk: explores a less familiar corner of the Downs. Derelict vehicles and locked churches indicate the proximity of the coastal towns.

Caution: there is no place of refreshment on this walk (see note on Piddinghoe). A descent can be made to Newhaven from Nore Down.

---

1. The first part of the route follows the SDW. From the Ouse bridge walk W through **Southease** to the main road (550m), cross and turn right. Cross the road to Telscombe and follow a path beside the main road down to a track (230m). Turn left and follow the track SW through the buildings of South Farm (1150m). Continue along **Cricketing Bottom**, turn left at the corner of a field (850m) and follow a track round a right-hand bend to a lane (500m). Follow the lane S into **Telscombe**, and take a track to the left of the church (400m).

2. Keep right at a fork (50m) and continue along a path. Join a track (600m) and continue E past houses on **Bullock Down**, the northern outskirts of **Peacehaven**. Where the track ends at the last house (600m) continue along a path through scrub. In a field turn right (100m) and follow its edge round to the left. Turn right through a gate (170m), follow a zigzag path down to a track and turn right (500m).

3. Walk W through **Halcombe Farm**, keep left at a fork (550m) and follow a metalled track uphill. At the top, where houses appear, take a path on the left (250m) and follow it E along the top of a field. At a corner, cross a stile (450m), turn right along a track and follow it SW past **Hoddern Farm** (350m). Follow the track round to the right and take a track on the left by a crumbling flint wall (300m). Follow the

Walk 30

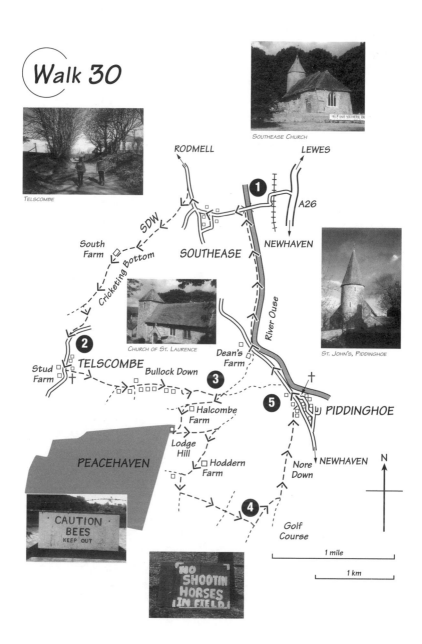

SOUTHEASE CHURCH

TELSCOMBE

RODMELL

LEWES

❶

A26

SDW

South
Farm

SOUTHEASE

NEWHAVEN

Cricketing Bottom

CHURCH OF ST. LAURENCE

River Ouse

ST. JOHN'S, PIDDINGHOE

❷

TELSCOMBE

Bullock Down

Dean's
Farm

Stud
Farm

❸

❺

PIDDINGHOE

Halcombe
Farm

Lodge
Hill

PEACEHAVEN

Hoddern
Farm

Nore
Down

NEWHAVEN

N

CAUTION
BEES
KEEP OUT

❹

Golf
Course

1 mile

1 km

NO
SHOOTIN
HORSES
IN FIELD

track round to the left by the corner of a field (200m) and at the next corner keep straight on (ESE) towards Nore Down.

4. Go down and then up into the scrub, turn left just past the corner of a field (1,000m), and follow a grassy path ENE along the flank of **Nore Down**. Exploration of the hill may involve encounters with golfers, motorcyclists, and tracks which terminate abruptly in impenetrable gorse. Continue along the top of a field with scrub on the right (300m) and then into open country (150m) and along the ridge, where there is a good view along the valley of the Ouse to Lewes. Join a track at the corner of a field, descend through farm buildings to **Piddinghoe** (1,150m) and cross the road. To explore the village, take a path opposite.

5. Turn left and walk NW along the road (900m). This stretch, a short-cut between Newhaven and Lewes, is not for the faint-hearted, but can be avoided only by a long detour towards Halcombe Farm (see map). Opposite a sign *Chapel Barn* (*Dean's Farm* on the map), cross a stile on the right, turn left, and follow a path N beside the **Ouse** back to the start (1,650m).

The Ouse near Southease

En route

Southease: a beautiful little village. ST PETER'S CHURCH is over 1,000 years old. Its unusual round tower may be due to the difficulty of building corners in flint. In 1604 the rector commented, after re-marrying a widower, "a shipwrecked sailor seeks a second shipwreck".

Telscombe: an unspoilt village, featured on the cover of the 1996 Explorer map, gives no hint of the proximity of PEACEHAVEN. Mercifully it has no through road. It was left to Brighton Corporation in 1933 on condition that it should not be developed. The CHURCH OF ST LAURENCE IS locked. STUD FARM has some massive old buildings. The MANOR HOUSE is XVI century.

Peacehaven: is generally held to be a sad example of uncontrolled development in the '20s and '30s. The buildings on Bullock Down show what could have happened elsewhere.

Piddinghoe: the CHURCH OF ST JOHN also has a round tower, with a weathervane in the form of a salmon trout (not a "dolphin", as Kipling wrote). If the map shows a public house it is out-of-date; THE ROYAL OAK has long been a private residence.

Oxteddle Bottom (Walk 31)

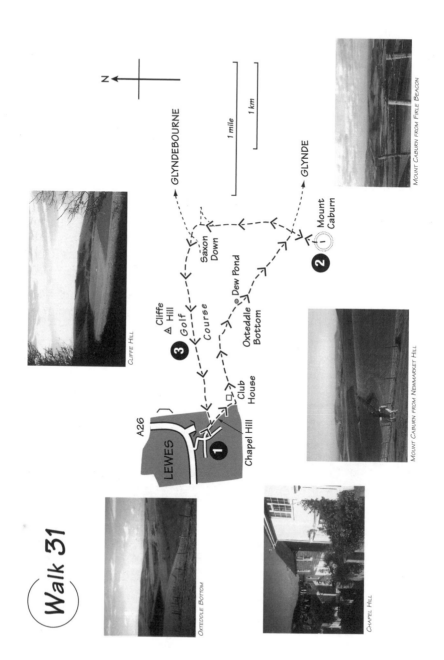

Walk 31

N

1 mile

1 km

GLYNDEBOURNE

GLYNDE

Saxon
Down

Cliffe
Hill

Golf

Course

● Dew Pond

Oxteddle
Bottom

2

1 Mount
Caburn

3

Club
House

A26

LEWES

Chapel Hill

CLIFFE HILL

OXTEDDLE BOTTOM

CHAPEL HILL

MOUNT CABURN FROM FIRLE BEACON

MOUNT CABURN FROM NEWMARKET HILL

Walk 31

Mount Caburn, Cliffe Hill

Distance: 7.0 km, 4.5 miles

Ascent: 225m

Time: 2:00

Maps: Explorer 122, Landranger 198

Parking: in Lewes, there are car parks and roadside parking near the Church of St Thomas à Becket at the junction of Cliffe High Street, South Street and Malling Street (m/r 421102). No parking is possible on Chapel Hill. There is no vehicular access from the south. From the roundabout on the A26 just N of the tunnel drive down Malling Street.

The walk: these hills form a separate island of downland, which often enhances the views from the main ridge. They give a short but excellent walk, which can be combined with a visit to Lewes. Shorter ascents of Mount Caburn are possible, but this is much the best.

---

1. From the church, walk SW up **Chapel Hill**, a steep, narrow lane. There is no *Chapel Hill* sign – look for a sign *Lewes Golf Course*. Continue up a private road to the clubhouse (550m) and walk round the edge of the car park to a stile (50m). Turn left along the hillside, with the car park initially on the left. Follow a path, which first contours the hillside ENE, and then descends to a stile (480m). Continue downhill (SE) above a steep slope and at another stile (200m) bear right and follow the path down into **Oxteddle Bottom**, which, although less than a mile from busy roads, can seem as remote and peaceful as a Highland glen. Join a grassy track by a dewpond (450m), and follow it round to the left along the bottom. Cross a stile on the right (300m) and follow a path SE up the hillside onto the ridge (750m). Turn right and walk to the summit of *Mount Caburn* (350m).

2. Retrace the outward route and continue N along the ridge, bearing round to the left just below the crest. Cross a stile by a gate (1,350m) and bear left along a grassy path where a track goes down to the right. The map may not show all the paths and tracks here. Cross a sunken track at its highest point (100m) and go uphill along a grassy track, which may not be shown on the map. Continue NW along the ridge and cross a stile just before the corner of a field (450m). The in-

viting path continuing towards the summit of **Cliffe Hill** is a dead-end. Follow a faint path which contours the hill-side, and continue WSW through another field (550m) to the golf course (220m).

3. The route across the golf course is not obvious. Look out for a series of waymark posts with warning signs affixed, which are just a little too widely spaced. Go just below a patch of scrub, cross open ground and continue through another patch of scrub. Bear slightly left, keeping the high ground on the right, and descend W towards Lewes, aiming for the castle. Descend to the edge of the course (1,000m), where the obelisk on the right (see below) may be visited by a short detour. Go steeply downhill along a path to **Chapel Hill** (150m), turn right and walk back to the start (180m). 1330 7130

En route

Lewes: is built on a hill, like Arundel. There is much to see, including LEWES CASTLE and the adjacent BARBICAN HOUSE MUSEUM (both open daily; tel: 01273 486290), of particular interest for artefacts excavated on the Downs; the ANNE OF CLEVES HOUSE MUSEUM (open daily 15 Feb- 7 Nov; some days at other times; tel: 01273 474610); SOUTHOVER GRANGE GARDENS (tel: 01273 483448), and the remains of LEWES PRIORY (tel: 01273 486290). There is a TOURIST INFORMATION CENTRE – see Introduction. Several good second-hand bookshops are an additional attraction.

Mount Caburn: (pronounced *Cawburn*) is a National Nature Reserve and, although there are few RoWs, access is permitted (Site Manager tel: 01273 476595). There is an Iron Age fort with massive ramparts on the summit, which is a splendid viewpoint for the eastern Downs and the Ouse valley.

Cliffe Hill: is a little higher than Mount Caburn, but the upper part is a golf course and, except for a solitary right of way which does not visit the summit, there is no public access. The obelisk seen on the right just above the houses is a memorial to 17 Protestant martyrs burned to death in Lewes during the reign of Queen Mary.